CONCILIUM

concilium 1995/2

THE MANY FACES OF THE DIVINE

Edited by
Hermann Häring and
Johann Baptist Metz

SCM Press · London
Orbis Books · Maryknoll

Published by SCM Press Ltd, 26–30 Tottenham Road, London N1
and by Orbis Books, Maryknoll, NY 10545

ISBN: 0 334 03031 5 (UK)
ISBN: 0 88344 88 3 (USA)

Typeset at The Spartan Press Ltd, Lymington, Hants
Printed by Mackays of Chatham, Kent

Concilium Published February, April, June, August, October, December.

Contents

Introduction:

The Many Faces of the Divine?

The topic and title of this issue prompt a discussion. In this age must we really talk about 'the divine' and must we really talk about 'many faces'? In a time of religious pluralization mustn't we speak of the *true face* of God? In a time of esoteric postmodernism and the new syncretism mustn't Christian theologians fight again dissolving *God* into an undefinable 'divine'? So doesn't the very theme succumb to a pressure of expectation contrary to the aims of a clear and binding faith in a God who offers the hope of a just messianic future? These warnings are justified. The danger to Western culture, manipulated by the media and psychological techniques, is no longer one of 'secularization' but of what J. B. Metz has called 'religion without God', and the Western interest in Eastern religions has often enough been motivated by a diffuse, dilettante interest in spiritual comfort and private stabilization.

But there is also another truth to which we have to turn at the end of this century, inter-religious communication. The world is growing together economically, politically and socially; the streams of media information have long ceased to recognize any national or continental limits. In the Western states, inter-cultural societies are developing for which Christian theology is not yet prepared, and the peace of the world will essentially be decided on the readiness of the religions to get to know and respect one another better. If, as the Second Vatican Council teaches us, God's truth is to be found in all religions, then we must also note that God is shown to us in amazingly many faces. Moreover, since many religious cultures feel that monotheistic talk of 'God' is an illegitimate limitation, for the sake of dialogue it must be permissible and possible to speak of the 'divine' in theological discourse. This 'divine' is not as remote from the Christian tradition as first impressions might suggest. On the contrary, we

Christians, too, know that we encounter our God only in fragments, in reflections and similitudes. Talk of the 'divine' need not necessarily lead to a dilettante attitude; it also signifies modesty, reverence and a readiness to learn from other religions.

This issue attempts to provide some initial orientation among the multiplicity of religious images of God. Such an orientation cannot be exhaustive, but with the help of selected examples and topics it can at least provide a framework of reference. It has three aims. The aim of the *first part* is to investigate the multiplicity of concepts, images and faces of God and the divine in the world religions. This part seeks primarily to describe, compare and indicate something of the inexhaustible multiplicity in which the religions approach the divine. Contributions on Taoism (Knut Walf), Hinduism (Angelika Malinar), Zen Buddhism (Ruben Habito), monotheism (David Tracy) and the doctrine of the threefold God (Hermann Häring) have been selected.

The aim of the *second part* is to provide some insight into basic dimensions of religious experience of God. The God of experience also has many faces. But the structures of religious experience at the same time seem to break through the linguistic and cultural straitjacket of individual religions and groups of religions. This part, too, is not only description but also analysis, and between the lines there are many surprises, appeals and questions, especially to the Christian tradition. Here we have reports of the Ntomba experience of God in Africa (Laurent Mpongo), and there is a presentation of a quite classical picture of Christian experience of God (Bruno Forte). A contrast is provided by the mystical theology of Meister Eckhart (Frans Maas) and the new impulses of feminist theology (Helen Schüngel-Straumann). Finally, a look into the symbolic world of the unconscious, into its individual and social significance, is cause for thought; these are themes which Drewermann has emphatically stamped on theological awareness (Peter Eicher).

But this multiplicity of offers and possibilities must also be ordered in some way. How are we to judge our experiences of God? How do they relate to the salvation and future of humankind, the battle against injustice and oppression? So the aim of the *third part* is to look at the praxis, in individual and social contexts, in which there is talk of God and religious action. In this third part norms are set. It will emerge what belief in God is ultimately about. What criteria are there for good and humane talk of God? How can we distinguish pseudo-religion from true faith? Do the monotheistic religions make a specific contribution to the question of the true God? The question arises in the face of the postmodern sense of life (Erik

Borgman) and a 'godless' society (Johannes Figl). An answer on the God of life and the gods of death comes from Latin America (Pablo Richard). This last contribution in particular can ensure that the inter-religious dialogue does not end in confusion, but gains in concentration.

Once again a discussion has been begun which will not end so quickly. But that not only accords with the now thirty-year-old tradition of *Concilium* but is also something which has happened often enough in the 'dogma' section, which for many years was the responsibility of Edward Schillebeeckx and Johann Baptist Metz and so has taken on an unmistakable form. Now Metz, too, has withdrawn from this work, and that marks the end of an era. From 1965 to 1972 he was responsible for the section on 'Church and World', from 1973 to 1979 for the section on 'Fundamental Theology' with Jean-Pierre Jossua and from 1980 for the 'dogma' section. I would like to thank him at this point in the name of countless readers from five continents. Johann Baptist Metz may be sure that we shall not squander his legacy, but profit from it for a long time.

Herman Häring

I · Images of God and the Divine

Tao – 'Treasure to the Good, Protection to Evil'

Knut Walf

I The teaching of Tao

Tao, a central concept in the ancient Chinese interpretation of the world, is usually translated 'way' in the so-called Western languages. And in Chinese or Japanese (*do*) Tao in fact means 'street'. But Tao is more; it has the abstract meaning 'teaching' or 'art'. Even more than in translations from other languages, the understanding, indeed the interpretation, of the translator becomes involved in translations from Chinese, especially of course if these are translations of abstract terms. The term Tao, too, is translated differently in Western languages, depending on the particular world-view of the translator. Therefore more and more translators prefer to leave Tao, this complex term, untranslated. Here are just a few examples of the way in which Tao has been translated (apart from 'way'): Logos, *natura naturans, ratio*, supreme Being, meaning, sense, law of the world, nature, providence, Reason, *cause première, nature, parole, principe, raison*.

The view that all that is has its origin in the unitary principle Tao is a commonplace in traditional Chinese thought. As a verb, Tao also means 'lead' or 'show the way'. The great Chinese sign dictionary of 1915 gives forty-six different meanings for 'tao'. 'Tao' is a concrete concept, but also – in Western language – an abstract philosophical and religious concept. In the context of Taoist teachings it means 'the way followed'. So there is also a temporal factor to it. The word also has an active aspect, for example in the sense of 'go one's way'. This leads to a further variant of Tao: the behaviour peculiar to each being. This form of Tao is in turn connected with the Tao which permeates everything, indeed forms a symbiosis. Tao is then the unitive principle of the whole cosmos. Tao is peculiar to each being and is at the same time Being.

The teaching of Tao is the basis for all religions and all philosophical and ethical trends or systems in ancient China. Its beginnings are obscure and lie in the prehistorical unconscious. In the age of magic Tao was presumably the name of the god of the ways. In the *I-Ching* (Book of Changes), presumably the oldest book to have come down to us complete (sixth, perhaps even seventh century BCE), Tao teaching is alive: behind change stands the immutable, imperishable Tao. Confucius also began from Tao in his ethical system. For him Tao is the principle of world order. Since the beginning of the twentieth century this 'commonality' has led to talk of a Chinese 'universism'; however, this view has rightly been refuted in recent times.[1]

At all events, the Chinese teaching of Tao on the one hand goes back before the time of Taoism and on the other also plays an important role outside Taoism. But as the name indicates, 'Taoism' is primarily based on Tao teaching. The early Taoists, the 'classics' of Taoism like Lao-tzu, Chuang-tzu, Lieh-tzu and Wen-tzu give the term Tao a more comprehensive meaning. In Western terminology Tao becomes a metaphysical concept. Lao-tzu especially sees Tao as a designation or better an indication of the nameless origin of all beings.

The most important Taoist book is by Lao-tzu, the *Tao-te Ching*, a book of comparable significance to the Bible; it may indeed be the most widely disseminated book of world literature after the Bible. It is said to have been written by Lao-tzu. Scholars even now have not established whether Lao-tzu is a historical or a legendary person. More recent scholarship assumes that the *Tao-te-Ching* was compiled around 300 BCE from probably very much older texts. The most significant Taoist book after the *Tao-te Ching* is by Chuang-tzu, and bears the title 'True Book of the Southern Land of Blossoms'. Chuang-tzu's dates are historically relatively certain (c. 350–300 BCE). The great books of Taoism also include that by Lieh-tzu, which bears the title 'The True Book of the Spring from the Primal Source'. Wen-tzu is thought to have been one of the direct pupils of Lao-tzu; in contrast to Chuang-tzu and Lieh-tzu he discussed Taoist teaching in a scientific way in keeping with his time. His work was recorded by his pupils. So here too we cannot establish any certain biographical dates (third century BCE?).[2]

Among the first people in the West to study the Taoist writings, especially Lao-tzu's *Tao-te Ching*, were Christian theologians, or at least lay people with a marked interest in theology.[3] The fact that in the West theologians or at least those interested in theology were among the first to concern themselves with Taoism and without any doubt furthered the spread of the Taoist classics led to interpretations of the terminology and content of the Taoist writings which gave rise to misunderstandings, and continue to do so.[4] A further danger was and is the temptation to want to discover parallels between Chinese and Western notions all too quickly. We find one of the most absurd examples in the history of the reception of Taoist writings in the West. A whole series of both nineteenth- and twentieth-century scholars wanted to see the name of the God of Israel, Yahweh, in chapter 14 of the *Tao-te Ching*. This was done with quite amazing acuteness and linguistic artistry. Victor von Strauss, who in 1870 published one of the first two German editions of the *Tao-te Ching*, in particular wanted to identify the words I (or Yi), Hi, and Wei (Weh), which occur there, as 'Yahweh'. Moreover he did not doubt that 'Tao' was a designation of the personal God in the Jewish-Christian revelation, so in his commentary on Ch. 14 of Lao-tzu he consistently spoke of 'Tao' without the article, whereas in his translation of the text he says 'the Tao'.[5]

II Tao – an apersonal principle?

Some scholars (G. Béky, Kah Kyung Cho, and others)[6] have compared Tao with the term *deitas*, which mediaeval theologians and mystics, especially Meister Eckhart, have used and which they put above God (*deus*). There are also similar notions in the concepts of other Western thinkers; one might simply mention the 'Ungrund' of Jakob Böhme or the 'Godhead' of Angelus Silesius. Now in fact Tao has predominantly an apersonal form, but in the Taoist classics there are also occasionally references to Tao with personal features. Thus for example it has feelings: 'Tao is good and faithful'.[7] In Chuang-tzu there is also a kind of invocation of Tao by the wise Hsu Yu:

'O my master! O my master! You destroy all beings in the world and yet you do not do justice. Your good deeds benefit thousands of generations and yet you do nothing that is well pleasing. You are older than the earliest age and yet you are not old. You protect the heaven and bear the earth. You shape and form all things and yet you do not do justice. That is the way of my master.'[8]

Lieh-tzu can say of Tao: 'It has no knowledge and can do nothing and yet it is all-knowing and almighty.'[9] And again Chuang-tzu: 'Tao does not act and has no form. One can hand it on without any other being able to receive it. One can understand it without being able to see it. It is its own root and has existed for ever, even before the creation of heaven and earth. Although it exists above the highest peak of the universe it is not high. Lying this side of the six ends of the universe it is not deep. Born before heaven and earth, it has no duration. Older than the oldest antiquity, it is nevertheless not old.'[10]

These few texts already show that despite all the personal features which are peculiar to Tao, it cannot be compared with the notions of God in the monotheistic religions. The attempts of the Taoists to explain Tao are free of any anthropomorphism. So we can also with good reason reject the view of some earlier researchers into or interpreters of Taoism (Dvorak, de Harlez, von Strauss, and others), that Tao can be compared with the personal God of Christianity or neighbouring religions. For unlike the prophets of Israel and most Christian theologians, and also unlike the philosophers of Greece who recognized the divine as eternal being,[11] for the Taoists Tao did not transcend the world. Everything is ultimately connected with Tao, issues from it and flows back to it. Everything not only partakes of the divine but also bears its character.

In the first chapter of the *Tao-te Ching*, in which he attempts to circle around Tao, Lao-tzu speaks of the 'primal mother of countless things' which Tao embodies. Lao-tzu depicts a bipolarity of Tao which is contrary to monotheism. This bi-polarity is not just the male-female opposition. The God of the monotheistic religions is a 'positive' God: his 'properties' are exclusively positive, so in the monotheistic religions evil remains an even greater mystery than God himself. By contrast, in the Tao-te Ching we have the enigmatic and provocative statement: 'The Tao – preserver of all things – is treasure to the good, protection to evil.'[12]

III Tao-being, non-being and cosmos

The Taoists supplement any statement about Tao, however careful, with another which is often completely opposed to it: 'The saying is often first true as an opposite.'[13] The Taoists characterize Tao, among other things, with the following two statements. Tao moves to and fro, keeps returning into itself, into the origin.[14] And, Tao is weak and simple like a small child or like the raw materials of nature.[15] Non-being, or the state which 'precedes' being, often preoccupied the Taoists. Thus for example we read in Chuang-tzu: 'If there is a beginning there is also a time when this beginning was not yet, and furthermore a time preceding the time when this beginning was not yet. If there is being, then non-being precedes it, and this non-being is preceded by a time, since even non-being had not yet begun."[16] The Taoist philosopher Wen-tzu was also deeply preoccupied with the question of the non-being of Tao: 'Tao forms and shapes all things without ever being corporeal. It is still and motionless, but it penetrates the chaos and the dark . . . Even if one divides it into its smallest particles, one still does not get within it."[17]

In all religions of West Asian origin the question of the ultimate ground of all being, of 'God', is closely connected with that of the beginning of the world and the origin of creation. Now it is striking that 'the problem of a possible "creation" hardly plays any role in Chinese thought'.[18] But particularly in the Taoist classics, especially in Lieh-tzu and Chuang-tzu, there are some very interesting theories about cosmogony and descriptions of it. These are theories which without doubt are based on very old oral traditions and therefore deserve special attention. So it is certainly attractive to compare the Taoist views on the connection between Tao and the 'first cause' with the doctrines of the monotheistic religions in particular. But in China, too, questions were evidently asked about a (personal) creator of the world, though this question may not have been a prominent topic, as it was in Western theology and philosophy (at least up to the Enlightenment). The question of the origin of creation is not raised as such in the *Tao-te Ching*, so there are no 'satisfying' answers in Lao-tzu. 'Nameless – the beginning of heaven, of earth', is how Lao-tzu puts it.[19]

IV Tao and God

After all that has been said about Tao so far, a Western reader may perhaps wonder about the relationship between Tao and God. Certainly I have already pointed out that Tao cannot be compared with the ideas of God in the monotheistic religions (Judaism, Christianity, Islam). It is occasionally claimed that the ancient Chinese had an 'equivalent' of God in the term 'Ti', and sometimes an analogy is drawn between Tao and Ti on the one hand and *deitas* (divinity) and *deus* (God) on the other. Ti was and is often translated 'God' in Western editions of the *Tao-te Ching* to the present day, for example in half the German editions, predominantly the earlier ones. Von Strauss even renders 'Ti' 'Lord'. It is the same with editions in other Western languages, and this is particularly marked in the English or American translations of the *Tao-te Ching*.

Now when 'Ti' is mentioned in connection with Tao in the *Tao-te Ching* we must of course understand it in the meaning which it had at the time when this text was presumably composed. At that time it was an equivalent for 'heaven', and heaven was personified as 'Shang-ti' ('Lord of Heaven'). However, Shang-ti in no way corresponds to the God of revelation in the faith and understanding of the three great West Asian religions. Presumably the Chinese did not know 'any completely pure theism'[20] before the invasion of Christianity (in the form of Nestorianism) and Islam. For in Shang-ti, while Ti was given human properties, it was not a personal being. The Taoists then stripped this Ti of its anthropomorphic features. Moreover in their commentaries on the *Tao te-Ching* the Chinese and Japanese interpreters hardly go into the two terms Tao and Ti at all. For them Ti is ultimately an unmythological term, moreover 'loaded' with popular religion. So Tao cannot be compared with Ti. And that Lao-tzu speaks of both only serves to describe the magnitude of Tao: 'Before Ti was, Tao was.' That should not exclude the possibility that Tao is also the philosophical transformation of Ti, for example along the lines of the philosophical and theological reflection of mediaeval Western thinkers which is evident in the two terms God-divinity (*Deus-deitas*).

After many years of studying Tao one will necessarily arrive at not so much the knowledge as the feeling that one can only have an inkling of Tao. To achieve this one also has to abandon the Western attitude, orientated as it is on knowledge. Zen is the best mediator of this attitude, having its origin in Chinese Chan Buddhism, which in turn represents a synthesis or symbiosis of Taoist and Buddhist thought. The Chinese Zen master Nan-ch'üan (748–834) put it like this; 'Where one has really achieved Tao, in which nothing is to be doubted, one is empty and alone, as in the open space of an enormous empty room, and no longer asks for yes and no.'

Anyone who goes in search of Tao must give up any idea of wanting to get knowledge about Tao. Accordingly, in East Asia no attempt is made, for example, to depict Tao in art, even symbolically, since there are subjective intimations of Tao which can only be objectivized by way of a beginning and are thus communicable. Certainly there is what is occasionally called 'didactic Taoism': for example, attempts at art including the making of gardens, sitting in silence or engaging in meditative movement (Tai-chi, etc) through which one can become open to Tao. For Tao is invisible, still, indeed even 'tasteless'.[21] Lao-tzu perhaps gives the briefest clarification of the difference between the West Asian concept of God and Tao:[22]

'Tao never wants to be master of things,
So one may call it great.

Because it does not measure its own greatness,
it can be great.'

Translated by John Bowden

Notes

1. Heiner Roetz, *Mensch und Natur im alten China*, Frankfurt, Bern and New York 1984.

2. Alfred Forke, *Geschichte der alten chinesischen Philosophie*, Hamburg ²1964, 333f.

3. Mention should be made first of the French Abel Rémusat. de Harlez, a Walloon, the American Edkins and the Germans von Strauss, Wilhelm, Grill and Schell should be singled out in this connection.

4. Thus it was Richard Wilhelm whose translations of Chinese classics still persistently influence their reception in the German-speaking world (and moreover there are translations of his translations into English, French and Dutch). He was a Protestant theologian who went to China as a missionary. Salome Wilhelm (ed.), *Richard Wilhelm – Der geistige Mittler zwischen China und Europa*, Düsseldorf and Cologne 1956.

5. Victor von Strauss, *Tao Te King*, Leipzig 1870; many editions followed e.g. that by Manesse, Zurich ⁸1987.

6. Gellért Béky, *Die Welt des Tao*, Freiburg and Munich 1972, 201f.; Kah Kyung Cho, 'Das Absolute in der taoistischen Philosophie', in *Transzendenz und Immanenz, Philosophie und Theologie in der veränderten Welt*, ed. D. Papenfuss and J. Söring, Stuttgart, Berlin, Cologne and Mainz 1977, 243.

7. *Chuang-tzu* VI.1.

8. Ibid., VI.6. Based on the French translation, *Philosophes taoistes*, Paris 1980. The French translation is by Liou Kia-hway and Paul Demiéville.

9. *Lieh-tzu*, I.3, following the translation by R. Wilhelm, *Liä Dsi – das wahre Buch vom quellenden Urgrund* (1911), Munich ⁴1992.

10. *Chuang-tzu* VI.1. Based on the French translation, *Philosophes taoistes* (n. 8), 130.

11. Peter Joachim Optiz, *Lao-tzu – Die Ordnungsspekulation im Tao te Ching*, Munich 1967, 192.

12. *Tao-te Ching* 62. My version of the text of the *Tao-te Ching* is taken from Ernst Schwarz, *Laudse, Daudedsching*, Leipzig ⁶1990.

13. Ibid., 78.

14. Cf. e.g. ibid., 25.

15. Ibid., 55 and 15.

16. *Chuang-tzu* II.6.

17. *Wen-tzu* I.3. Cf. Forke, *Geschichte der alten chinesischen Philosophie* (n. 2), 337.

18. Béky, *Die Welt* (n. 6), 131.

19. *Tao-te Ching*, 1.

20. Alfred Forke, *Die Gedankenwelt des chinesischen Kulturkreises*, Munich and Berlin 1927, 38.

21. *Tao-te Ching*, 35.

22. Ibid., 34.

God, Gods and Divinity in the Hindu Tradition of the Pāñcarātra

Angelika Malinar

Different theological and philosophical terms are used to elucidate the dimensions of divine presence in the traditions of Hinduism. The multiplicity of religious traditions and theological systems makes a systematic account difficult. Furthermore, the term 'Hinduism' as a religious or theological category is by no means certain. It does not appear in the classic texts and traditions which are regarded as witnesses to this religion; rather, it was coined in the early nineteenth century by Christian missionaries and European scholars to denote the different Indian religions.[1] With it a great variety of religious practices, philosophical traditions and regional cults were brought under the same heading, and historical and systematic differences were often neglected. The problem of this unification emerges when, for example, one attempts to give a general account of *the* concept of God, *the* theology or *the* ritual practice of Hinduism. Accounts differ depending on the choice of texts on which they are based. There is no basic text which holds for all traditions (as, for example, the Bible does), no 'creed' binding on Hindus and no 'church' which is an institutional representation of faith as a whole.[2] On the other hand, to dispense completely with the term 'Hinduism' and to limit oneself to depicting individual traditions in isolation can have the disadvantage of bracketting off fundamental features which the different traditions have in common. These common features arise not least from discussions between individual religious groups at several levels. These discussions document not only the differences but e.g. in the theological sphere also a consensus on particular themes which must be covered in a theological system and the terminology used for explaining them. This legitimates the attempt to discuss God and divinity in Hindu traditions in a systematic way. For this purpose the historical and regional characteristics of individual traditions must be relegated to the background and their value as examples be stressed. The divine being is discussed in the different Hindu schools under aspects that can be systematized. I shall describe these aspects and investigate them by means of texts from the Viṣṇuitic Pāñcarātra tradition.[3]

Before doing that, however, I shall indicate the historical context which has shaped the structure of the concept of God that can be termed 'Hindu'. In terms of the history of religion 'Hinduism' can be said to be the result of the social and religious developments which took place around the third century BCE in the process of demarcation from Buddhism and Jainism and also from the ancient Vedic sacrificial religion. At this time a concept of God was developed which also shaped later theology. The postulate of a concern to preserve the world order by means of a supporting ritual was taken over from the Vedic traditions. At the same time, as e.g. in Buddhism, the quest for redemption from the cycle of death and birth (samsāra) and the connection between action and result was elevated to become an aim. The doctrines of the individual soul, the 'self' (atman), formulated in the literary genre of the Upanishads (from the sixth century BCE), are particularly important for the concept of redemption. While this self is entangled in the consequences of its actions (karman), because it participates in the origin of all that is visible (brahman), it is immortal and is to be redeemed. As the 'supreme Self' God now becomes the guarantor of redemption.

Early witnesses to this development are the Bhagavadgita (c. first century BCE) for Viṣṇuism and the Śvetāśvatara Upanishad for Śivaism. He alone is to be worshipped ritually, and in him alone is redemption to be sought. In subsequent centuries this doctrine of God is developed in the Purāṇa literature and from around the sixth century in the Saṃhita (Viṣṇuitic), Āgama (Śivaitic) and Tantra (Śāktistic) texts.[4] This God is characterized on the one hand by his being redeemed and by the tranquillity of his divine consciousness and on the other by his concern for the well-being of those in the world. Thus the divine being develops in two respects: on the one hand God is unchangeable being, the supreme soul and completely free. On the other God makes the world come into being, sustains it and brings about its downfall. The question why an immutable consciousness causes the visible variety of the world or why a world created by God is full of suffering was raised time and again by critics of the doctrine of God. The conceptual tensions which are implied in the characterization of divine being and those in Christian theology, for example in the question of theodicy or the problem of the relationship between divine freedom and divine perfection, also become a topic in the Hindu traditions.

I God as the supreme self (*paramātman*)

At the highest level the divine being is pure consciousness and has no bodily manifestation (*amūrta*). God is the soul which is already redeemed, free from the conditioning which characterizes the existence of the individual soul. At this level there is only a single supreme consciousness, only a single all-embracing God. As there are many and varied Hindu traditions, this God who occupies the supreme position is given different names. Three main traditions can be distinguished, depending on the supreme deity and the theology connected with this deity. 1. For the Viṣṇuitic schools, Viṣṇu, Kṛṣṇa or Nārāyaṇa occupies the supreme position; 2. For the Śivaites, Śíva or Paramaśiva is the supreme god; 3. In the Śāktist tradition it is the goddess Śakti, Devī, Durgā or Kālī. The schools use a similar terminology to characterize this supreme deity. It is pure consciousness (*caitanya* or *cit*), true being (*sat*), happiness (*ānanda*) and complete independence (*svātantrya*):

> ‘“God (*bhagavān*) is like the cloudless heaven, like the unmoved sea – God is a great sea of pure, fully independent consciousness, of being in truth and happiness, completely free from all limitations by form of manifestation, place and time” – that is how one is to recognize the supreme, unchangeable self (*paramātman*)’ (*Lakṣmī-Tantra* 7.2–3).

What term or group of terms becomes particularly relevant for a school and what interpretation is given usually depends on the philosophical definition of the ‘self’ (*ātman*) which underlies the theological system.

For example, in a description of the ‘supreme Self’ in a text from the Viṣṇutic Pāñcarātra school, the transition from ‘unchangeable being’ into a becoming is interpreted as a process of consciousness:[5] ‘The supreme self whose distinguishing characteristic consists in a passionless, boundless happiness, *is* – the wise see those places beyond, peculiar to him . . . The “I” whose form is completely unlimited is called the “supreme Self”. This all – what is conscious and what is unconscious – is embraced by it’ (ibid., 2.1.4). There is then a description of how the ‘I’ of the deity becomes the ‘self’ which appears in all beings. The formation of the world begins in the appearance of the supreme self as an ‘I’. Once the condition of ‘I-being’ is realized, there is immediately a ‘this’ (*idam*), and the first fundamental difference has come about in the unchangeable being. If the 'I' realizes its 'I-ness', the divine creative force (*śakti*) is aroused. In the *Lakṣmī-Tantra* the goddess Lakṣmī is the 'I-being' (*ahaṃta*) and the creative power of the god Hari-Nārāyana. 'I' and 'I-being', creative force and the 'illumination' of the consciousness, are inseparably connected. The god Nārāyaṇa and the goddess Lakṣmī form a couple. On a logical level their relationship is interpreted as a concomitance (*avinābhava*): they cannot be without each other. In the Śivaitic traditions, too, Śakti is often depicted as the female side of the god in the form of a goddess. In Viṣṇuism she can also be made subordinate to the *brahman*,[6] a special cosmogonic sphere which unites the divine constituents in itself. Thus the divine consciousness is related to a creative force in which all that is visible is already potentially present. The conception e.g. of a *creatio ex nihilo* therefore plays no role in the Hindu doctrine of God.

II God as author of the manifest world

The creative power of God or God's 'I-being' is realized in the origin, existence and passing away of the world. Here the individual soul's power of knowing is veiled, but the god at the same time becomes the guarantor of its redemption. When the god turns to the creation of the world, the individual cosmological instances come into being in a process of emanation. The emanation of the world is divided into two (or even three) phases. In the first phase the *śakti* develops its potential on a subtle level. This phase is described as *śuddha* (pure) or *para* (beyond). According to the Pāñcarātra it consists in the development of the six constituents (*ṣaḍ-guṇa*) of the divine being:[7]

1. *Knowledge* (*jñāna*) is God's real form of being and shapes the other constituents: 'Enlivened, knowing itself, eternal, embracing all things in itself – that bears the name of knowledge.'

2. The *creative force* (*śakti*) is what becomes the material foundation and primal form (*prakṛti*) of the visible world.

3. *Ruling power* (*aiśvarya*) denotes the completely unlimited capacity of God for action.

4. *Strength* (*bala*) is shown in the fact that God is not exhausted in the activity of creating the world.[8]

5. *Steadfastness* (*vīrya*) is the immutability of God, even in creating the world.

6. *Splendour* (*tejas*) is the divine self-sufficiency, God's independence from any support (*sahakāryanapekṣā*).

The 'supreme Self' is designated Vāsudeva when these constituents rest in it undeveloped. The six guṇa form three pairs which shape the character of three further divine forms: knowledge and strength become the god Saṃkarṣaṇa; ruling power and steadfastness become Pradyumna; and creative force and splendour become Aniruddha. The group of the four gods is called '*caturvyūha*', the 'four formations'. Each *vyūha* has a specific creative force which is represented by a goddess. When the wish is aroused in Vāsudeva to create the world, his *śakti* develops into the three other *vyūha*. Then the supreme immutable consciousness-being (*kūṭastha-puruṣa*), which is omniscient and contains all individual souls (*jīva*) in itself, comes into being from Pradyumna. The social stratification, the so-called 'caste system', consisting of four states, is already contained in him. The creative power related to this *puruṣa* is called *māyā* – the creative power which keeps the souls from redeeming knowledge. The *māyā* activates the three potential limits on the individual souls entering the world:

1. *Niyati*, i.e. the limitation or definition: 'What kind of a form it (the individual soul) can have, what kind of action (and) what its specific disposition may be . . . all this is produced by the (power) of determination' (*Ahirbudhnya-Saṃhitā* 6.48).
2. Time (*kālā*), as the temporality which conditions all actions, drives the individual souls towards their determination.
3. The *guṇa-māyā*. This creative force consists of three *guṇa* which are to be distinguished from those mentioned above. They form the material foundation of the visible world. They are called *sattva*, *rajas* and *tamas*. The range of meanings for these concepts covers spheres which are separate in Western understanding. They denote both natural phenomena and moral and spiritual qualities.

For this reason, several translations are given here: 1. *sattva* is light, lightness, clarity, happiness; 2. *raja* is unrest, passion, grief and dust; 3. *tamas* is darkness, stupidity, heaviness, apathy. From the constant transformation of these constituents arise among other things intellectual capacity, the sense organs and the elements. In the hierarchy of divine manifestations these three constituents are aspects of the fourth *vyūha*, Aniruddha. They are represented by three gods: Viṣṇu watches over the *sattva* and the ongoing existence of the world order (*sthiti*), Brahma sees to all activities in creating the world (*sṛṣṭi*) which are involved in *rajas*, and Rudra as ruler over *tamas* is responsible for the standstill and ultimately the downfall of the world (*saṃhāra*).

The second phase of the creation of the world, which is called 'unclean' (*aśuddha*) or lowly (*apara*), begins with Brahmā. This phase consists in the emanation of cosmological matter, including the senses and the elements. The description of this phrase is relatively homogeneous in the various schools. The individual souls enter into a body which corresponds to their prior life. Good and evil deeds have particular effects which can extend into the next life in the form of 'maturings' (*vāsanā*). 'Not-knowing' is an unchangeable element of any creation of the world 'without a beginning'; the 'concealment' of knowledge (*tirobhava*) is part of the divine action. However, the divine grace (*anugraha*) can help the individual soul to redemption through the different ways of salvation and the manifestations of God in the world which are connected with them.

III Divine manifestations in the world

Different motives are given in the texts for the manifestation of the divine creative force as world: the desirability of a divinely protected world order, the divine game (*lila*), or the granting of a possibility of redemption for the souls. For example, the *Lakṣmī-Tantra* puts particular emphasis on the motive of helping: creation is desired in order to help beings to salvation, i.e. to do away with their ignorance. This ignorance is 'without beginning' and an unchangeable element of divine action. One sign of ignorance (*avidyā*) is the entanglement of beings in the actions which result from their wishes. In order to open up a possibility of redemption for beings, God appears in particular forms of manifestation. These on the one hand ensure the ongoing existence of the world order as a whole, and on the other support individual souls on their way to redemption. These divine forms are subdivided into three groups:

1. The *four forms of manifestation* (*mūrti*) of the *catur-vyūha* group, mentioned above. Thus as well as having a cosmogonic function, the *vyūha* group also has a soteriological task: to help individuals on the way to redemption. To this end the manifestations assume a specific form (*mūrti*) which is clearly characterized in iconography. They can be visualized and evoked by meditative practices. However, that is possible only if one has been initiated into the practices (*sādhanā* or *yoga*) of the particular traditions. Thus we read in the *Lakṣmī-Tantra* (19.17): the supreme form (*pararūpa*) of this *vyūha* group is 'venerated by those who have succeeded in the practice of Yoga, in their hearts'.

2. The *thirty-eight* or *thirty-nine vibhavas* appear for the well-being of the world (*jagathita*) and have a specific task (*kārya*) to fulfil. In these 'descents' (*avatāra*) the god appears in either a divine or a human form.

The mythological side of the god can be recognized in the list of *vibhavas*. Thus numerous *vibhavas* are given the task of killing demons or other adversaries of the divine order. So these forms of manifestation are connected above all with their actions in preserving the world. Accordingly, their veneration is related to their functions within the world.

3. *The arcā forms* are divine images in the temple, which are venerated in accordance with the ritual prescriptions of the particular school. Part of the divine creative power (*śakti*) or divine consciousness (*caitanya*, *cit*) is present in these divine images. So in the temple ritual believers can make direct contact with these gods in order to have their wishes fulfilled: 'The form of god which was made for the well-being of the worlds of gods, wise men, ancestors, successful ascetics and so on, or which has taken shape by itself, is the temple image (*arcā*) which consists of pure consciousness' (ibid., 4.31). The multiplicity of gods in the Hindu traditions has its roots in the distribution of ritual competences. At this 'lower' level of the one divine being one can speak of a 'polytheism'. This distribution of ritual competences among different gods also made possible, historically speaking, the integration of gods from other traditions or regional cults. Both the iconographized *vyūha* forms and the *vibhava* can be venerated as divine images in the temple.

The relationship of the divine forms of manifestation to the well-being and also the state of knowledge of the individual soul becomes clear in the following passage from the *Lakṣmī-Tantra* (11.41):

> [The goddess Sri Lakṣmī said]: 'The manifestations of God or the gods in accordance with the division into his supreme *vyūha* form and so on arise as a demonstration of favour towards the individual soul and out of compassion for those who worship him with great devotion.' [Indra, king of the gods, said:) 'Honour to you, O goddess, the darling of the god of gods, the lotus-born! Only a single form should be enough for showing favour to his followers!' [The goddess Sri Lakṣmī said]: 'The accumulations of merits are different in individual souls. Individual souls by no means accumulate (their merits) at the same time . . . Through the gradations of merit there are differences among those who have a ritual entitlement.'[9]

Moreover individuals have different capacities of knowledge. The different forms of manifestations come into being in order to do justice to these differences. Those who have trodden the way of Yoga successfully are justified in turning to the highest form of the deity. But those who through the practice of yoga want not only to come nearer to redemption but also to improve their situation within the world should turn to the *vyūha* forms. If the knowledge of redemption is still not very developed, then the veneration of the *vibhava* and *arcā* forms is advised.

Thus the multiplicity of divine manifestations is in no conflict with the unity and uniqueness of God and God's creative power. Rather, it takes account of the social and soteriological position of individuals. The difference is determinative of the creation of the world which emanates from God. Thus as well as the triad of the creation (*sṛṣṭi*), preservation (*sthiti*) and destruction (*saṃhāra*) of the world, the veiling (*tirobhava*) of redemptive knowledge in individual souls and the showing of favours (*anugraha*) which can further both redemption and well-being within the world belong in the sphere of the dimension of God which is turned towards the world. The five divine activities are summed up as *pañcakarman*.

IV The downfall of the world in God

The existence of the world is bound up with a temporal rhythm. So periodically there is a 'downfall of the world', i.e. the gradual reabsorption (*saṃhāra*) of the world. The dissolution of the world takes place through a reversal of the stages of its creation. The individual cosmological elements return to their origin: the creation of the world is the cosmic day, the 'opening' of God's eyes (*unmeṣa*) which ends in the cosmic 'night' (*rātrī*), the closing of the eyes (*nimeṣa*). The principle of this reabsorption becomes clear in this description of the dissolution of the elements:

> 'The water swallows up the essence of the earth, its smell . . . If the earth is robbed of its smell it immediately loses its name and form. Then the water takes possession of the whole world . . . Fire, as the cause [of the water] swallows up the essence of water, the taste . . . If the water is robbed of its taste it immediately loses its name and form. The world is only a flaming fire' (*Ahirbudhnya-Saṃhitā* 4.15ff.).[10]

However, the dissolution of the ingredients of the cosmos only goes as far as a certain stage, so that the world can never come to a final end; the dissolution ends with the entry of the above-mentioned three *vyūha* into Vāsudeva. So the reabsorption does not affect the supreme divine being, God as the 'supreme Self'. Only the individual soul can come into contact with this sphere, and be redeemed in it. However, in so doing it goes through the same stages of emanation in the opposite direction. For the world as a whole, however, there is no redemption nor a final downfall in the form of an apocalypse.

V God as the place of redemption

Because the determination of the essence of the divine being and the being of the individual souls correspond to each other, redemption is possible. In most of the above-mentioned traditions the performance of rituals and meditative or ascetic practices serve as means (*upāya*) to redemption. Thus according to the *Lakṣmī-Tantra* (15.17), the 'wishless' fulfilment of ritual duties which are an obligation because of membership of a particular social stratum are such a means. Otherwise the rituals serve to fulfil personal wishes and at the same time contribute towards the preservation of social order. They become a possibility of redemption if one renounces one's wishes.[11] Only then does the ritual become exclusive worship of the supreme God. The way of meditation consists in a gradual approach to the different divine forms of manifestation, reversing the course of cosmology. Here the divinity is represented by a meditative visualization of the iconography of the god and by the evocation of the divine form with the help of a 'mantra'. A 'mantra' is a combination of sounds or syllables which correspond to particular aspects of the divine being or even a whole divine figure.[12] By the recitation of these syllabic formulae one comes into contact with the deity and can appropriate this dimension of the divine consciousness. For this way of 'realization' (*sādhanā*), an initiation into the doctrinal tradition of the particular school is necessary. Both means are orientated on the different above-mentioned divine manifestations, which are a sign of divine grace towards individual souls.

However, there is yet another 'demonstration of favour' which is based on a personal relationship between God and the individual. The love of God (*bhakti*) is an element which is an essential constituent of the 'Hindu' doctrine of God. In the framework of *bhakti* the inclination of a believer to God is associated with participation in the destiny of his follower. A further possibility of redemption which has become part of the traditions on which this account is based has its foundation on this concept: the presupposition of redemption can be created by a single act of grace on the part of the god or goddess. This can happen by the divine power spontaneously falling upon the individual soul. The 'descent of the divine creative power' (*śaktipāta*) is usually attributed to the goddess. She is seized by compassion for souls tormented in the cycle of death and birth and spontaneously frees them from the veiling of their power of knowledge

(*Lakṣmī-Tantra* 13.3–11). The goddess declares: 'Now I alone know the moment of the descent of my divine power. This moment cannot be brought about by human efforts or by any other cause.' At this moment the soul recognizes that it is truly pure consciousness (*cit*), and from now on works to establish this knowledge. When the soul has purged itself of all stains it shines and becomes identical with the divine consciousness. Then it no longer returns to the world.[13]

Concluding comment

Despite the multiplicity and complexity of the theological and religious traditions of Hinduism, there is a consensus over what aspects of the divinity must be ingredients of the doctrine of God. For this reason it was possible to undertake a systematic description of these aspects, and the Viṣṇuitic Pāñcarātra tradition was used as an example. The unity of the divine consciousness and its freedom as the 'supreme self' constitutes the supreme sphere of divine being. In it alone redemption is possible for the individual soul. If the divine consciousness becomes 'I', it is necessarily related to its creative power (*śakti*). The *śakti* develops its potential for action in favour of individual soul by seeing to the origin, continuation and passing away of the world. By the veiling of its capacity for knowledge the individual soul is entangled in the divine world order. But in this world, at the same time the grace (*anugraha*) of God is present in the form of its manifestations and as a result of the diverse possibilities of redemption. The supreme self, pure consciousness, is attained when the individual soul leaves the world and recognizes itself as part of the divine being. However, God can be known only if the souls stay in the world and turn to the divine forms of manifestation as signposts towards their own salvation.

Translated by John Bowden

Notes

1. See Wilhelm Halbfass, *Indien und Europe*, 1981, and Heinrich von Stietencron, 'Hinduism', 1991.

2. The Veda, the earliest collection of hymns and ritual texts, cannot be regarded as such a basic text. The Vedic 'revelation' is made the authoritative foundation of the theology of the later schools even when the content of this theology is remote from the Veda. The acceptance of the Veda as 'revelation' is certainly a link between the Hindu schools over against the Buddhists who do not accept it. However, we are not to infer

any theological or ritual unity from this. See J. C. Heesterman, *Die Autorität des Veda*, 1974.

3. For a survey of the textual tradition see F. O. Schrader, *Introduction*, 1916.

4. For a survey see Ludo Rocher, *The Purāṇas*, 1986, and Teun Goudriaan and Sanyukta Gupta, *Hindu Tantric and Śākta Literature*, 1982; also Madeleine Biardeau, *L'Hindouisme*, 1971, and ead., *Études de mythologie hindoue*, 1981.

5. The *Lakṣmī Tantra* was composed around the tenth or eleventh century. At some levels the text shows links with the theology of the Śivaite schools in Kashmir, the heyday of which was between the ninth and the twelfth centuries. In other interpretations (leading to a dualism) the transition from the unity of the divine being to a multiplicity is interpreted as a process of 'ontological loss', so that the multiplicity of the world is to be seen as unreality.

6. The term *brahman* points to the rooting of this theology in the Upanishad tradition, where at countless points the *brahman* is mentioned as the place of the world's origin.

7. For what follows cf. *Ahirbudnyasaṃhita* 2.54–61 and *Lakṣmi-Tantra* 2.27–36.

8. This contrasts e.g. with the Vedic tradition, according to which the creator of God is exposed to a loss of power which makes ritual feeding necessary.

9. The word *adhikāra* denotes the (ritual) entitlement which each person has depending on status or level of initiation. The form of initiation and access to the temple ritual is primarily determined by the caste to which a person belongs.

10. The following stages of emanation are a basis here: wind → fire → water- → earth.

11. This doctrine of action 'without wishing' is first presented in the Bhagavadgita. It served above all to bridge the contrast between ritual tradition and the doctrine of redemption.

12. For details see André Padoux, *Vāc*, 1993, and Gerhard Oberhammer, *Strukturen yogischer Meditation*, 1977.

13. Another interpretation of this act of grace is mentioned at another point of the *Lakṣmī-Tantra* (ch. 17), the so-called *śaraṇāgati* (or also *prapatti*), 'taking refuge in God'. Here God reacts to the complete surrender of the believer. Cf. *Lakṣmī-Tantra* 17.60–62.

Bibliography

Ahirbudhnya Saṃhitā of the Pāñcarātra Āgama, edited by M. D. Rāmānujācārya under the supervision of F. Otto Schrader (2 vols.), Madras 1916.

Biardeau, Madeleine, *L'Hindouisme. Anthropologie d'une civilisation*, Paris 1971.

—— *Études de mythologie hindoue. I. Cosmogonies Purāṇiques*, Paris 1981.

Gonda, J., *Die Religionen Indias*, Stuttgart 1978.

Goudriaan, T., *Gupta, Sanyukta: Hindu Tantric and Sākta Literature*, A History of Indian Literature 2.2, Wiesbaden 1981.

Halbfass, W., *Indien und Europa. Perspectiven ihre geistigen Begegnung*, Basel and Stuttgart 1981.

Heesterman, J. F. C., 'Die Autorität des Veda', in Gerhard Oberhammer (ed.), *Offenbarung: Geistige Realität des Menschen. Arbeitsdokumente eines Symposiums zum Offenbarungsbegriff in Indien*, Vienna 1974.

Lakṣmī-Tantra. A Pāñcarātra Āgama, edited with Sanskrit gloss and introduction by Pandit V. Krishnamacharya, Madras 1959.

Lakṣmī-Tantra. A Pāñcarātra text, translation and notes by Sanjukta Gupta, Leiden 1971.

Oberhammer, G., *Strukturen yogischer Meditation*, Vienna 1977.

Padoux, A., *Vāc. The Concept of the Word in Select Hindu Tantras*, New York 1990.

Ludo, R., *The Purāṇas*, Wiesbaden 1986.

Schrader, F. O., *Introduction to the Pāñcarātra and the Ahirbudhnya Saṃhitā*, Madras 1916.

von Stietencron, H., 'Hinduism: On the Proper Use of a Deceptive Term', in Günther D. Sontheimer and Hermann Kulke (eds.), *Hinduism Reconsidered*, Delhi 1991, 11–27.

Zen and Human Existence

Ruben L. F. Habito

It must be noted at the outset that Zen[1] Buddhism is non-theistic, that is, not at all concerned with the notion of God or with the question of God's existence or non-existence. Its central concern, as that of Buddhism in general, is rather the resolution of the fundamental problem of human existence, characterized in this tradition as *dukkha* (unsatisfactoriness).

We must therefore clarify that our task in this article is not to cull out of Zen Buddhism some notion of or doctrine about God. It is rather to engage Zen Buddhism in conversation, and to listen intently and carefully to what it has to offer in terms of its understanding of our *human existence*. Based on such careful listening, we can then offer some reflections for Christians engaged in a *theo*-logical endeavour.[2]

This article consists of two parts: the first examines key elements of Zen praxis and the Zen way of life; the second offers *theo*-logical reflections on implications of the Zen life for a Christian understanding of God.

I Zen: the awakened life

Zen defines itself with a fourfold set of characteristics said to come from *Bodhidharma*, the bearded ascetic depicted in many Zen paintings, who brought this way of meditative practice from India to China around the sixth century of our common era. These characteristics are enshrined in the following verse:

'Not relying on words or letters, (it is)
A special transmission outside of Scriptures,
Pointing directly to the human mind,
Seeing one's nature, being awakened.'[3]

It is thus repeatedly emphasized that Zen is not a doctrine or a philosophy that can be presented and accounted for in verbal and conceptual terms, but rather a praxis and way of life centred on the experience of 'seeing one's (true) nature', and thereby 'being awakened (= becoming a Buddha, or awakened one)'.

1. Emptying of ego-consciousness

The crux of this way of life is the practice of seated meditation, or *zazen*. *Zazen* is the locus wherein we can uncover all that Zen is about, the fulcrum of an awakened life. It involves sitting (either on a cushion or low chair) with one's back straight, legs folded, eyes open, and in this posture, breathing deeply but regularly, letting one's mind come to rest in the here and now. Its pivotal point is in the emptying of the ego-consciousness, casting off that mode of thinking that divides our being into subject and object, seer and seen, hearer and heard, thinker and thought, self and the other, as well as all the other oppositions we find in our life: birth and death, pleasure and pain, good and evil, here and there, now and then. In other words, in *zazen*, the practitioner enters into a process that culminates in total self-emptying. As one's praxis ripens, the above-mentioned oppositions are overcome, and one arrives at a state of pure awareness (*samadhi*). Such a state of awareness is also called 'non-thinking' (Japanese *hi-shiryo*). It must be noted, however, that this state is not to be mistaken for absent-mindedness, absolute passivity or loss of consciousness. On the contrary, it is one that involves a total engagement in one's sitting. This much can be gleaned from the following passage, from the writings of Dogen, a Japanese Zen Master of the thirteenth century:

'Once, when the Great Master Hung-tao of Yueh shan was sitting (in meditation), a monk asked him,
"What are you thinking, (sitting there) so fixedly?"
The master answered, "I'm thinking of not thinking."
The monk asked, "How do you think of not thinking?"
The master answered, "Non-thinking."'[4]

We will not go into the technicalities involved in the longstanding debate on this matter of 'non-thinking', and will simply note that it is neither 'introspection', wherein the subject turns inwards but still in a way that thinks of mental objects, nor the stopping of mental faculties. Rather, in this state of awareness, one overcomes the normal subject-object modal way of thinking, and one arrives at an awareness of pure be-ing.

2. *Return to the concrete world*

This awareness of pure be-ing is not something that happens in a vacuum, but in and through the very concrete historical conditions surrounding one's *zazen* practice, that is, sitting here, legs folded, back straightened, eyes open, breathing in and breathing out, in this room (or wherever the sitting may be taking place) at this given point of time. In short, it is not an 'out of body' experience, but a very much embodied event rooted in the historical realities of one's being. And yet, at this very place, in this very moment, all the boundaries of space and of time collapse, as there is no 'subject' standing, or sitting, *vis-à-vis* a given objective place, and no time before or time after that a given subject can measure or tally.

With the emptying of the ego-consciousness, the 'object' that one is normally conscious of is also emptied, and thus there is no longer anything 'out there' to be seen, nor heard, nor smelled, nor tasted, nor touched. There is absolutely 'nothing out there' any more, and there is 'nothing in here' to look out and see.

This experience of emptying of one's ego-consciousness opens out to an entirely *new dimension* to which no verbal description can do justice (cf. 'not relying on words or letters'). Yet again, as noted above, it does not take place in a vacuum nor in an extra-terrestrial realm, but in one's concrete historical embodiment, here, now. As such, it is an experience that goes full circle in a second 'moment', with a recovery of this concrete, historical, embodied way of be-ing.

The following exchange throws light on the above:

'Joshu earnestly asked Nansen: "What is the Way?"
Nansen answered, "The ordinary mind is the Way."'[5]

The Zen Master *Yamada Koun (1907–1989)* explains:

'It is nothing but . . . our ordinary everyday life. It is just getting up, washing your face, eating breakfast, going to work, walking, running, laughing, crying; the leaves on the trees, the flowers in the field, whether white, red or purple. It is birth, it is death. That is the Way . . .'[6]

But there is a difference: it is no longer getting up, washing one's face, etc., in the way we would do these ordinary actions under the governance of our ego-consciousness. The leaves on the trees, the flowers in the field, etc., are no longer 'out there' as objects of our consciousness. Rather, 'getting up', 'washing one's face', etc., become the consummate expressions of that pure awareness of be-ing, emptied of all ego-consciousness, yet embodied in concrete historical reality. 'Leaves on the trees', 'flowers in the field', etc., *emptied of their objectivity*, emptied of the perceiving subject, likewise are experienced as the concrete manifestations of pure be-ing itself, unobjectified, unsullied, unparalleled, just as they are.

3. *Ocean of compassion*

'Zen enlightenment' thus involves a 'moment' of emptying of the ego-consciousness, and a 'moment' of return to concrete historical reality (i.e. from that 'empty' vantage point, that 'awareness of pure be-ing'). These, however, are not separate events following one another in a linear time frame, but, although distinguishable, can be simultaneous and instantaneous.

Many things remain to be said concerning this key experience that defies words or letters, but one important aspect must be noted to cap our brief treatment. Of those who have taken that full circle, the following is said: 'Why is it that the crimson lines of a clearly enlightened person never cease to flow?'[7] 'Crimson lines' is another way of expressing 'tears of compassion', and this terse statement describing the fully enlightened person captures the heart of the awakened life as culminating in a third 'moment': the barrier that divides Self and Other having been broken, one awakens as bathed in a bottomless ocean of com-passion (literally, 'suffering-with'), with every single breath finding oneself at-one with all sentient beings in their suffering. This ocean of compassion is the matrix that nourishes an awakened one, and empowers one to engage in concrete tasks in the historical world.

II The faceless, triune reality

Needless to say, the Zen way of life and praxis depicted above does not at all refer in an explicit way to the notion of God, nor does it need its invocation in its articulation within the Zen tradition. Our question then is, what can we learn from the Zen way of life and praxis that can throw some light on a possible understanding of Christian existence, wherein the notion of God *is* so vital and central?

Addressing this question, let us look to the three 'moments' in the Zen life described above, as a basis for further reflection in this regard. The first is the emptying of the ego-consciousness, the second is the return to the concrete world of historical reality, and the third is the awareness of being bathed in the ocean of com-passion.

1. Unknown and unknowable

The first 'moment' in Zen praxis is the plunge into a realm that on the one hand is emptied of the ego as grasping subject, and on the other, is emptied of all possible objects to grasp. This is described in the initial declaration of the *Heart Sutra*, a short text that is said to succinctly capture the gist of enlightenment and is recited or chanted in centres of Zen practice: 'Form is no other than Emptiness'. This realm is described on the one hand as a state of *total blindness* (from the 'subject' point of view), and on the other, also as a state of *total darkness* (from the 'object' point of view). It is thus entry into a realm that is ultimately unknown and unknowable (that is, in so far as 'knowledge' implies 'a grasp of some objective reality by a conscious subject'). If God-talk is to make any sense in this context, it is God as ultimately unknown and unknowable, unobjectifiable, un-image-able, and which no verbal description nor conceptual formulation can ever approach. It is an unfathomable realm, 'too deep for words',[8] a realm that is, echoing Augustine, *intimior intimis meis* (more intimate to me than I am to myself).

2. Enlightened as a 'new creation'

But if one only dwells in this realm, then one is for ever lost into the unknown, unable to see nor speak, or even move at all. It is the second 'moment' that makes possible the *real-ization* of the Zen experience in the historical world: here one comes full circle and returns to the very concrete reality of one's embodied being, in the here and now. At this juncture, the second declaration of the *Heart Sutra*, which immediately follows the first, is understood: 'Emptiness is no other than Form.' In other words, the realm of emptiness comes to take a concrete *historical and tangible shape and form*, whether it be a colour such as a brown patch on the wall, or a sound such as the sneeze of someone nearby, the pain in one's legs, etc. In this 'moment', the divine darkness comes to light and manifests itself in the ordinary mind, in 'getting up, washing one's face, eating breakfast', as well as in 'leaves in the trees', 'flowers in the field', etc. But there is a difference: one experiences each event, each aspect of one's ordinary life, from its ground in emptiness, that is, as *'enlightened* by the divine darkness'.

This 'difference' is echoed *in Paul's exclamation* in Gal. 2.20: 'I live, no longer I, but Christ in me.' And following this lead, we can get a glimmer of the inner life of such a one: in Pauline terms, plunged into the mystery of Christ's death-resurrection, having died to one's self (ego-consciousness), one now lives in the newness of life, in all that one is and does. Emptied of self, arriving at that realm which is beyond all knowledge, one comes to be filled with the utter fullness of God (cf. Eph. 3.18–19). Everything, and every moment, is experienced as a new creation, partaking of the fullness of the mystery of being *'in Christ'*.[9]

3. *Suffering-with all*

In the third 'moment', with every breath, one awakens in the depths of the ocean of com-passion, identifying with the suffering of all sentient beings. In Christian terms, to live the newness of life 'in Christ' is also to live as suffering-with all of those embraced by Christ on the cross. Thus, with every breath, as one is filled with the newness of life in Christ, one is also bathed in the ocean of com-passion, the very Spirit of Christ, identifying with the pain of all those who suffer. This com-passion is what empowers one to engage oneself in concrete ways toward the alleviation of that suffering, to make concrete decisions in this light and take on the tasks in one's given historical situation.

III At the inner circle

Summarizing the above, the three 'moments' in the Zen awakened life open our eyes to a triune Reality that is at the very *heart of Christian existence*. It is 'triune', that is, it is threefold, and yet at the same time it is one and the same Reality. The 'three-fold' consists, first, in the Unknown and Unknowable which is also the unfathomable Source of all (John 1.18; 6.46); second, in the One wherein all things come to be and come to be, fully manifest and embodied in concrete historical reality (John 1.14); and third, in the Ocean of com-passion that sustains and unites the whole of creation, that gives and fills it with life (Gen. 1.2; John 6.63). This 'three-fold' is the one and same Reality that is both the 'ground' as well as the 'fulfilment' of Christian existence.

'Faceless' would be an apt way of describing this triune Reality of Christian existence: there is no way one can conceive of it, in any of its three 'moments', as an 'object out there' (i.e. *vis-à-vis* oneself as a subject). Rather, one simply awakens to one's true self as right at the heart of this triune Reality, the Unknown, the Manifest, and the Ocean of Compassion. In other words, one does not see its 'face', as one is situated right at the very *inner circle* of its dynamic Life.

'To recover one's original Face'[10] (a Zen expression which means to awaken to one's True Self, the key to the overcoming of the unsatisfactoriness (*dukkha*) that characterizes this earthly existence), thus, is to real-ize oneself at the very bosom of this faceless, triune Reality, with every breath, at every moment of one's life.

Notes

1. *Zen* is the Japanese form for the same ideogram also pronounced as *Chan* (Chinese), *Son* (Korean), or *Thien* (Vietnamese).

2. For the methodological presuppositions involved in conversation with other religious traditions as a resource for Christian theological inquiry, cf. F. X. Clooney, *Theology After Vedanta: An Experiment in Comparative Theology*, New York 1993.

3. Cf. R. Habito, *Healing Breath: Zen Spirituality for a Wounded Earth*, New York 1993, 21–37, for documentation.

4. Dogen's 'Lancet of Seated Meditation' (originally in Japanese). Translation in C. Bielefeldt, *Dogen's Manuals of Zen Meditation*, Berkeley 1988, 188–9; original in D. Okubo (ed.), *Dogen Zenji Zenshu* 1, Tokyo 1969, 90–101.

5. K. Yamada, *The Gateless Gate*, Tucson 1990, 93.

6. Ibid., 94–5.

7. Ibid., 99. Part 3 of 'Shogen's Turning Words', in *Miscellaneous Koans* used in the Sanbo Kyodan Zen lineage, No. 15.

8. Cf. T. Hall, *Too Deep for Words*, New York 1988.

9. Cf R. Habito, *Total Liberation: Zen Spirituality and the Social Dimension*, New York 1989, 1–9, for further development of this theme of the awakened life 'in Christ'.

10. For the Zen anecdote in which this expression appears, cf. R. Aitken, *The Gateless Barrier*, San Francisco 1990, 147–54.

The Paradox of the Many Faces of God in Monotheism

David Tracy

I Monotheism and its different meanings

The first problem with monotheism is the word itself. Although its basic meaning is clear (*monos-theos*: the one-God) that meaning changes into a surprising multiplicity as the horizon for understanding the word 'monotheism' shifts. Wittgenstein's insistence that meaning is not an abstract property of words but is discovered by noting the *use* of a word in a context is nowhere more true than in a case like the word 'monotheism'. It is the ever-shifting contexts that change the meaning.

1. Context: Enlightenment

At least three contexts are worth noting here. First, 'monotheism' is a modern philosophical word meaning an abstract property (oneness) that belongs to God alone. More exactly, 'monotheism' is an Enlightenment invention (H. More, D. Hume) that bears all the marks of Enlightenment rationalism. Monotheism, in this not so secretly evolutionary view, is a contrast word to 'polytheism'; i.e. (by Enlightenment standards) monotheism is a more rational understanding of the logic of the divine as implying a unicity of divine power, not a dispersal of that power into many gods and goddesses. Like the other famous 'isms' of the Enlightenment (deism, pantheism, theism, panentheism), modern philosophical 'monotheism' is, above all, 'rational' and 'ethical'. The relationship of this Enlightenment notion of monotheism to the historical religions (especially but not solely Judaism, Christianity and Islam) is often obscured by Enlightenment prejudice against 'positive' (i.e. historical) religions in contrast to 'natural religion'. Unfortunately most philosophical and even many theological uses of the word 'monotheism' still bear this dehistoricized and decontextualized Enlightenment meaning.

2. *Context: history of religions*

A second context also presents itself for understanding the word monotheism – history of religions. In a history of religions context 'monotheism' is a category employed to describe the 'family resemblances' among different religious phenomena: the 'high gods' of some primal traditions (e.g. the *deus otiosus* traditions in Africa); the philosophical reflections of the logic of unicity among the Greek thinkers from Xenophanes to Aristotle, a possible name for some Indian thinkers (especially Ramanujan); a clear name for such religions as Sikhism and Zoroastrianism; the revisionary monotheism of the reforming pharaoh Akhenaton; above all, of course, the three classical 'religions of the book', or, in history of religions terms, the historical, ethical, prophetic monotheism of Judaism, Christianity and Islam. Clearly such 'history of religions' reflections have influenced modern scholarship on the history of ancient Israel as well as the history of early Islam.

Many scholarly studies show the final emergence of radical monotheism in the 'Yahweh alone' prophets (especially Amos, Elijah, and Hosea). This movement culminated in the prophet of the Babylonian exile (Deutero-Isaiah). There Yahweh is clearly not only the God of Israel but also both creator of the whole world and the one and only God who determines not only Israel's history but all history: recall Deutero-Isaiah's reading of the Persian king Cyrus as the 'Messiah' appointed by Yahweh. It is the Deuteronomic reading of Yahweh which will influence the theological – i.e. radical monotheistic – reading of Israel's history in the Bible. From that point on, the central religious affirmation of Judaism, Christianity and Islam will be the classic *shema Yisrael* of Deuteronomy 6.4–5: 'Hear, O Israel: The Lord our God is one Lord; and you shall love the Lord your God with all your heart, and with all your soul, and with all your might!'

The route to this radical monotheism, however, was a long and complex one whose many twists and turns are still debated among scholars. Indeed, there are few more fascinating debates in the history of religion than the conflict of interpretations among scholars of ancient Israel on the most likely history of the emergence of radical monotheism from polytheism, henotheism, monarchic monotheism and monolatry. There can be little doubt that, in the emergence of radical monotheism in ancient Israel, there have been as many forms for the divine reality as there were names for the divine power(s).

In strictly historical terms, radical monotheism is a relatively late arrival in the founding history of ancient Israel. But the principal theological question of today for Jews, Christians and Muslims is not so much the theological implications of the fascinating history of the earlier different names and forms for the divine in the complex history of ancient Israel but rather the still contemporary theological question of the different forms for the experiencing, naming and understanding of divine reality since the prophetic and Deuteronomic emergence of radical monotheism.

3. Context: theology

Hence, the third and, for present purposes, principal context for understanding the word monotheism is the strictly theological context of the category for monotheistic Judaism, Christianity and Islam. For the purpose of clarity, this theological-soteriological understanding of historical ethical monotheism bears the following characteristics:

1. God is *one*: an individual distinct from all the rest of reality.
2. God is the *origin*, sustainer and end of all reality;
3. God, therefore, is the One with the *person-like characteristics* of individuality, intelligence and love;
4. God, and God alone, is related to all reality. Indeed God is *Creator* of all reality both natural and historical;
5. In sum, God, and God alone as the Wholly Other One, is both *transcendent* to all reality and totally *immanent* in all reality;
6. God *discloses Godself* in chosen prophets, historical events and scriptures.

II Islamic and Jewish monotheism and the many faces of God

1. Islam

Among the three historical radically monotheistic religions, Islam has been the most insistent on the centrality of the oneness of God. The monotheism of Islam is not only a soteriological monotheism but a profoundly dogmatic one. Indeed, the dogma of the oneness of God (*tawhid*) is the central dogma of Islam. This absolute otherness of God is kept alive in every form of Islamic practice and thought. But this Islamic insistence on God's transcendence is never to be misinterpreted (as unfortunately it still is by secular and even Christian thinkers) as implying the remoteness or distance of God from humankind. Indeed Islam's genius for keeping God's transcendent oneness (and thereby otherness) the central dogma in all Islamic life has provided a rich sense, not of remoteness, but of the closeness and presence of God in Islamic life and thought.

Islam (precisely as a word meaning 'surrender to God') has a great theological hermeneutics of suspicion upon all forms for representing Allah, since any form might obscure God's total otherness and transcendence, i.e. God's oneness (*tawhid*). Of the three radically monotheistic religions, Islam is the most hesitant in encouraging different 'faces' of the divine. Above all God's oneness must never be compromised. At the same time, as the great Islamic mystical traditions (especially, but not solely, the Sufis) as well as the sheer beauty of the stark forms of Islamic art and culture show, Islamic radical monotheism has its own ways – mystical, artistic, theological piety – to portray the many faces of the One God.

2. *Jewish thought*

This openness to many forms of the divine is even more the case in the other two radically monotheistic religions, Judaism and Christianity. Indeed, probably the richest theological discussion today of radical monotheism is the extraordinary debate in Jewish thought. Consider the great range of modern and post-modern Jewish options here: the insistence from Moses Mendelssohn to Herman Cohen and many contemporary thinkers in the Reform tradition that Judaism is quintessentially 'ethical monotheism'; the complex existential categories for divisions within God occasioned by God's relationship to human suffering in F. Rosenzweig; the reflections of both God's 'absence' and God's presence in every I-thou relationship in M. Buber; the great recovery of the many diverse faces of the one God in the mystical, especially kabbalistic, traditions of Judaism recovered by G. Scholem through M. Idel and so many other contemporary scholars; the new post-Shoah 'mad midrash' reflections on the faces of God (E. Fackenheim and E. Wiesel); and the new covenantal orthodox Jewish theologies on the disclosures of God in history (D. Harman). One cannot but be struck by the amazing vitality, proliferation and intense conflict of interpretation on how to interpret Judaism's profoundly monotheistic understanding of God.

To summarize some of the most important aspects of this great monotheistic tradition: From the classical Jewish insistence never to name G_d, through the debates (at once rabbinic and modern philosophical) on Jewish 'ethical monotheism', through F. Rosenzweig's reflections on the *shema Yisrael* and *shekinah* that takes place within God as God gives Godself to the people Israel, to the intensely mystical and daringly speculative understandings of the very material letters of God's names in kabbalah, therefore, the question of the many faces of the one God has returned with explosive and creative force in contemporary Judaism.

3. A religious category

In Judaism, Christianity and Islam, monotheism is a religious before it is a philosophical category. Indeed, even within theology itself, soteriological monotheism is older than and grounding to all dogmatic monotheism. For the Jew, the Christian and the Muslim, monotheistic faith is fundamentally a gift of God: God's gift of self-revelation. Philosophical discussions of monotheism are indeed welcome and often relevant (e.g. for issues of credibility and intelligibility) in strictly theological analyses of religious monotheism. But for Jewish, Christian and Muslim believers monotheism is fundamentally gift, grace, faith: *credere Deum Deo* – to believe in God through God's own self-revelation: in the covenant with the people Israel; in the Qur'an given to the prophet Muhammad and in Jesus the Christ.

III Christian identity of God and the many faces of God

1. God in Jesus Christ

To understand the many faces of the divine in Christianity means to understand who God is in and through the revelatory event which is, for the Christian, the decisive mediation, as self-revelation, of God: the person of Jesus Christ. A Christian understanding of God becomes the question of the identity of God: Who is God? For the Christian, God is the One who revealed Godself in the ministry and message, the cross and resurrection of Jesus Christ. A Christian theological understanding of God cannot ultimately be divorced from this revelation of God in Jesus Christ: neither through solely philosophical understandings of 'monotheism' (although these philosophical arguments are, of course, relevant for questions of intelligibility); nor through historical-critical reconstructions of 'the historical Jesus' (although these reconstructions, even if never constitutive of Christian self-understanding, are relevant as corrections of traditional views – e.g. Docetic, Monophysite and merely traditionalist christologies).

The full Christian doctrine of God discloses the many faces of divine reality that must inform every symbol and doctrine just as the doctrine of

God is informed in its many faces by every symbol and doctrine (creation-redemption, eschatology, church, spirit, sacrament, revelation and especially christology). A theological insistence on the interconnection of the central mysteries of the faith is true, of course, of the understanding of every great symbol of Christian faith, but is especially crucial on the question of God and the many faces of the divine. Christian theology must always be radically theocentric, so that no single symbol or doctrine in the whole system of doctrines can be adequately understood without explicitly relating that symbol to the reality of God as disclosed in Jesus Christ.

2. Passion narratives – New Testament

The passion narratives, nicely described by H. Frei as 'history-like' and 'realistic', disclose the most basic Christian understanding of not only the identity of Jesus Christ but, in and through that identity, the identity of the God who acts with the 'face' of the divine agent in and through the actions and sufferings of Jesus of Nazareth. As in any realistic narrative, so too in the passion narrative, an identity is rendered through the plotted interactions of an unsubstitutable character (Jesus) and the unique events (betrayal, cross, resurrection) which Jesus both performs and suffers. The fact that the Christian understanding of the one God is grounded not in a general philosophical theory of monotheism but in this concrete passion-narrative history of God's self-disclosure as agent in the cross and resurrection of Jesus of Nazareth is the primary theological foundation of all properly Christian understandings of God and the many faces of God.

The passion narrative, moreover, should not remain isolated from the rest of the scriptures nor from the later creeds. Rather, the passion narrative, as foundation and focus of all properly Christian understanding of God, should open up to the larger Gospel narratives on the message and ministry of Jesus, the theologies of Paul and John, the Pastorals, the Book of Revelation, and all the rest of the New Testament. The many faces of God, for the Christian, are found, therefore, not only in the foundational insight into God's 'face' as principal agent in the passion narratives and thereby in all history and nature.

God is also disclosed through the pre-passion actions of the ministry and message of Jesus of Nazareth as they are rendered in importantly different ways in the four Gospels. The typical speech of Jesus, for example, becomes part of the way through which Christians understand the many faces of God: the parabolic discourse on the reign of God discloses God's face as an excess of both power and love (e.g. the Prodigal Son); the typical word of Jesus for God, Abba, becomes crucial for any Christian understanding of the power ('Lord') and mercy (Father) of the mysterious face of God disclosed through Jesus; the centrality of the cross in the apocalyptic tale told by Mark and the dialectical language of Paul also opens later Christians to the *tremendum et fascinans* face of God disclosed in the hidden-revealed God of Luther, Calvin, and Pascal; the intrinsic link of Jesus' actions to the poor, the oppressed and the marginal especially in Luke and Mark open many Christians to discovering the face of God above all in the faces of the victims of history and all those involved in the prophetic struggle against all oppression.

3. Old Testament – God is love

At the same time, as focussed and grounded in the understanding of God's agency in the passion narrative, the Christian understanding of God should also open to the complex and profound disclosures of God's identity in the history of Israel rendered in the many genres (narrative, law, praise, lamentation, wisdom) of the Old Testament. This is clearly not the place to review and interpret the *extraordinary complexity* of a full scriptural understanding of the many faces of God disclosed in the many scriptural genres to name God. This much, however, does need to be affirmed: for the Christian, God is above all the One who disclosed the authentic face of God in raising Jesus of Israel from the dead. God, for the Christian, is the One who revealed decisively who God is in and through the message and ministry, the incarnation, cross, and resurrection of none other than Jesus the Christ.

The most profound Christian metaphor for the true face of God remains the metaphor of I John: God is love (I John 4.16). To understand that metaphor (which occurs, let us note, in the first theological commentary on the most theological and meditative of the four Gospels), is to understand, on inner-Christian terms, what has been revealed by God of God's very identity as agent and as the very face of love in the ministry, the message, the incarnation, cross and resurrection of Jesus Christ.

The answer to the question 'Who is God?', therefore, for the Christian faithful to the self-disclosure of God in Jesus Christ, is: God is love and Christians are those agents commanded and empowered by God to love. However, if this classic Johannine metaphor 'God is love' is not grounded in and thereby interpreted by means of the harsh and demanding reality of the message and ministry, the cross and resurrection of this unsubstitutable Jesus who, as the Christ, discloses God's face turned to us as love, then Christians may be tempted to sentimentalize the metaphor by reversing it into 'love is God'. But this great reversal, on inner Christian terms, is hermeneutically impossible. 'God is Love': this identity of God the Christian experiences in and through the history of God's actions and self-disclosure as the God who is love in Jesus Christ, the parable and face of God.

To affirm that 'God is love' is also to affirm, now, in the more abstract terms proper to post-scriptural metaphysical theologies, that the radically monotheistic God, the origin, sustainer and end of all reality, is characterized by the kind of relationality proper to that most relational of all categories, love. God, the One Christians trust, worship and have loyalty to, can be construed, in more abstract terms, as the radically relational (and, therefore, personal) origin, sustainer and end of all reality.

4. *Trinitarian monotheism*

To affirm that the Christian understanding of God refers to the One whom Christians worship, trust and are loyal to is also to 'place' this Christian understanding on the language-map of radical monotheism (shared by Judaism and Islam). To affirm, with I John in and through the Gospel narrative and the ecclesial confession of the incarnation, cross, and resurrection of Jesus Christ, that 'God is love' is further to affirm the radical relationality of God's nature as ultimately mysterious yet person-like (i.e. characterized by intelligence and love). The latter affirmation, moreover, both grounds a theological understanding of the economic Trinity in the primary Christian confession of Jesus Christ and also suggests how the immanent Trinity can be understood in and through the economic Trinity.

Christian monotheism is a trinitarian monotheism. For the trinitarian understanding of God is the fullest Christian theological understanding of the radical, relational, loving, kenotic God who revealed Godself in and through the incarnation, the ministry (healing, preaching, actions), the name 'Abba' for God and the parables on 'reign of God', the fate of the cross and the vindication of the resurrection of Jesus of Nazareth and the disclosure of this Jesus as the Christ through the power and activity of the Spirit. It is impossible to separate theo-logy and christology. In that same sense, the Christian understanding of the 'existence' and 'nature' of the radically monotheistic God must be grounded in the 'identity' of the God disclosed in the many faces suggested by the history and effects of Jesus Christ. Each of the three classical radical monotheistic traditions finds its own route to the many faces of the one God. The Christian finds that route in and through the many faces of the one God disclosed decisively through the Spirit in Jesus Christ, the face of God.

Bibliography

For further information and bibliography, see:
Concilium, Volume 177, *Monotheism*, ed. Claude Geffré and Jean-Pierre Jossua, 1985.
Frei, Hans, *The Identity of Jesus Christ*, Philadelphia 1975.
Lévy, Bernard-Henri, *La Testament de Dieu*, Paris 1979.
Ludwig, Theodore M., 'Monotheism', in *The Encyclopedia of Religion*, ed. Mircea Eliade, Volume 10, New York 1975, 66–136.
Moltmann, Jürgen, *The Trinity and the Kingdom of God*, London and New York 1981.
Niebuhr, H. Richard, *Radical Monontheism and Western Culture*, New York 1960.

Christian Belief in the Threefold God

Hermann Häring

'. . . and baptize them in the name of the Father, and of the Son, and of the Holy Spirit' (Matt. 28.19).

The literature about Christian belief in the triune God would fill libraries. It began in the second century and is still in full flood.[1] All the great theologians have written on the subject. But because of inter-faith dialogue the discussion has entered a new stage. In this article I shall be demonstrating what possibilities for misunderstanding, perhaps illegitimate provocations, belief in the threefold God contains. But we shall also see what legitimate challenges the image of the threefold God can produce for inter-religious dialogue. Finally, I hope to show how this disputed doctrine, peculiar to the Christian tradition, points to the ineffability of the divine, which resists all attempts to fix it in some way. We shall move towards this conclusion in four steps: first a critical diagnosis, then an account of the original Christian impulse, then some theses on the triadic structure of the divine, and finally a new interpretation of the symbol of the Trinity which may prove acceptable in inter-religious discussion.

I Critical diagnosis: a series of misunderstandings

The image of God in Christian faith has paradoxical features. On the one hand Christians believe clearly and unconditionally in a personal God. This God created heaven and earth, and by providence governs the world; God has history and us human beings in his hands; at the end of times God will prove himself to be the Lord even over evil and death. Christian faith shares this view unconditionally and without qualification with Judaism and Islam. On the other hand Christianity has the image of a threefold

God. As is well known, this does not mean a belief in three Gods. But we Christians believe in a God 'in three persons', to use the terminology laid down in all the mainstream Christian churches. So there are three persons in one God; God is three in an undiminished sense. At the same time all three persons are the one God; so these three are one in an undiminished sense. This doctrine has always been described as an impenetrable mystery; even the numbers 'one' and 'three' are to be understood only in an analogous sense.[2] But no final reconciliation of the statements has ever been achieved. According to the classical doctrine of the Trinity God is threefold and triune, depending on where the emphasis is placed.

1. Paradoxical and unsatisfactory

All down the centuries this has remained a paradoxical and unsatisfactory definition. It remains paradoxical, since divine unity and personal trinity form a tension which has never been clarified rationally without remainder and therefore has constantly led to misunderstandings. The contrast between unity and trinity has always been a thorn in the flesh of the understanding. At the same time the definition has remained unsatisfactory; for while many impressive explanations were given in scripture and early tradition, they were never completely convincing.[3] Belief in the triune God cannot be understood in terms of its biblical origins without any break. Certainly there was talk of a fundamental triad at a very early stage. The metaphors of God's 'son' and 'spirit' are deeply rooted in the biblical tradition. The baptismal command in Matthew speaks of 'Father', 'Son' and 'Holy Spirit' (Matt. 28.19). Paul ends a letter to Corinth with a tripartite formula, 'The grace of the Lord Jesus Christ and the love of God and the fellowship of the Holy Spirit be with you all' (II Cor. 13.13). And finally Father, Son and Spirit form the central principle of division in the Apostles' Creed: 'I believe in God the Father Almighty; I believe in Jesus Christ; I believe in the Holy Spirit.' These three are always mentioned alongside or after one another. But there is no reflection whatsoever on the fact that they are all divine, nor on their unity of substance in a more precise philosophical way, nor on a concept of threeness within the Godhead.

On the contrary, in the New Testament 'God' (Greek *ho theos*) always means, clearly and without any hint of differentiations within the Godhead, the one God who will tolerate no other gods alongside him.[4] Jesus called him 'Abba', 'Father', and Christians may confidently call him 'Abba' (Matt. 11.27; Mark 14.36; Gal. 4.6). So to begin with there is no trace of a doctrine of the Trinity. The new development began only when Christian faith gradually lost its Jewish context and became part of Hellenistic culture, i.e. Hellenistic thought and Hellenistic piety.[5] The decisive connecting link ran through the great turning point in christology which became the great catalyst of trinitarian thought. From the Council of Nicaea (325) on, Jesus might be called 'true God'. This terminology was to continue from then on, although 126 years later at the Council of Chalcedon, as a deliberate paradox the phrase 'true man' was added. The same has been true of the Holy Spirit since the First Council of Constantinople (381). He too is 'true God', now 'created' by God like earthly things, within time. These statements about the 'Son' and the 'Holy Spirit' set out the framework. It was to remain a very stable framework, although these definitions mobilized a comprehensive conceptual apparatus, whole thought-systems – especially in the fourth and fifth centuries.[6] Where is the critical point in this development which causes us such difficulties today within Christianity and in interconfessional dialogue?

2. The danger of tritheism

The theological problems were already known in the nineteenth century, and today they are no longer denied by any leading theologians. But they did not lead to an unqualified repudiation of the notion of the Trinity: that would be hermeneutical nonsense.[7] However, we can no longer take over the theories of the Trinity from history without any differentiation. As early as 1960 Karl Rahner warned against an unexpressed Christian tritheism.[8] This danger has still not been banished. Our prophetic roots, the biblical impulses which are profoundly monotheistic, can often no longer be recognized. No wonder that we also risk misleading others into thinking that we believe in three Gods and are promptly accused of blasphemy. The discussion between Judaism and Christianity fixed on this question at a very early stage. The Jewish exclamation was soon ignored: 'Hear, O Israel, Yahweh is our God, Yahweh alone!'

This saying has been constantly emphasized in the history of Jewish theology.[9] Belief in three 'persons', above all in the divinity of Jesus, would thus contradict the basic approach of belief in Yahweh. It would be unacceptable for Judaism to identify a human being with him, the one God of the Fathers. Islam was later to react with comparable decisiveness. It will never tolerate any doubt in the divine, inexpressible unity of the All-Merciful: 'God is but one God. God forbid that he should have a Son' (Surah 4.171).

3. A special Christian doctrine

Of course these answers, too, can give rise to avoidable misunderstandings. The doctrine of the Trinity in its original form did not seek to replace the biblical message, but to interpret it. The problem began when people forgot the tension between Jewish and Christian thought that the doctrine of the Trinity had to balance out. Now it turned into speculation and finally called for great intellectual efforts. Now – and this is the most striking characteristic – it produced a great discrepancy between rational abstraction and religious experience. No wonder that finally the idea of three figures (iconographically, for example, two human beings and a dove) simply swept aside all differentiations within theology and with this simplicity finally came to govern the Christian image of God.

Does the notion of the threefold God still have any public significance? In his article in this issue David Tracy points out that the modern discussion of monotheism takes place in three contexts. The context of Christian theology is characterized by a transition. On the one hand the classical trinitarian theology is deeply rooted in all denominations; but at the same time new forms of theology and piety have come into being in which the image of the threefold God hardly survives. Philosophical communication about the threefold God is now rootless, and has virtually no connections with the modern question about God. Finally, in the context of the phenomenology of religion, belief in the threefold God is noted only selectively, as a special Christian development.[10] In a phase in which the great religions are asking new questions about God together, the specifically Christian doctrine of God thus risks becoming dissipated. Many Christian theologians have joined this stage of the discussion willynilly. Sometimes they yield to the pressure of the arguments and simply stress the one and only God, of Christian faith as well; sometimes they have the naive view that we must first agree on the one God: then we could add belief in the threefold God as a Christian supplement.

So all that is left is a move forward. It is necessary to go on the offensive in presenting the specifically Christian image of God and relating it to the images of God in other religions. Here two levels of analysis emerge. The one level is that of historical development; we could call it the genealogical level. At this level no claim to absoluteness can be made, simply for reasons of historical contingency. The second level of that is the theoretical one of reflection on symbols, but on this level results must be aimed at which are also significant for the other religions.[11]

II Father, Son and Spirit: the original triadic impulse

As I have already indicated, this critical diagnosis is not being made in order to bid farewell to faith in the threefold God, but in order to rescue it from the polarization between 'traditional' and 'progressive' thought. Indeed, it is striking that the critics of the doctrine of the Trinity who have existed at all times are regularly overwhelmed by a broad stream of trinitarian piety. From what truth does this piety draw its force? It is also striking that the defenders of the doctrine of the Trinity, who have also existed at all times, have kept causing misundertstandings and have had to take refuge in abstract intellectual constructs. At what point have they gone beyond their limits? Finally, it is striking that the triad of Father/ Mother, Son and Spirit has taken on a new significance in social theologies and theologies critical of culture, one which by no means impedes inter-religious dialogue. Whereas Scholastic and later university theology had concentrated on statements about being, now the praxis of Christian faith is returning to the centre.[12]

Now this simple praxis of faith already existed in Christianity before the theology of the Trinity, and from the beginning was anchored to three elementary fixed points. At a moment which was critical politically, socially and culturally, a committed group of Jewish women and men, inspired by the rabbi Jesus, discovered in a new way what God meant for them in this praxis, what Jesus' messianic project meant to them, and finally what it meant for them for God to be present in the here and now.

This new discovery led to new and unusually rich experiences.[13] They are summarized and formalized in the Apostles' Creed as belief in the 'Father', the 'Son' and the 'Holy Spirit'.

1. Trust

We begin with belief in 'Yahweh', the God of Abraham, called 'Father' in Christianity and 'Allah' in Islam. He, the 'Lord', the 'Almighty', the 'All-merciful', 'Mother', 'Governor' and 'Creator of all things' is the basic symbol behind all the Abrahamic religions. Here they have found their common root and here the decisive quality of the prophetic religions is crystallized. God is worshipped as the one *person* towering over all things, and human beings are imagined as being God's image and likeness. This imagination[14] is shaped by the experiences that human beings have been chosen by God, that they have been given a goal, and that they can accord with God's will. It is a relationship of unconditional loyalty and unconditional trust, which makes it possible even to love one's enemy and to confront suffering. Like Jewish and Muslim faith, Christian faith, too, keeps referring back to this radical beginning;[15] it is not without reason that the basic religious attitude is understood as 'trust' and 'loyalty'. God is an inexpressible 'You' in whom are all things, who has created us and to whom we shall return.

We know that this trust and this loyalty can take many forms. It involves openness and expectation, commitment and dedication. In between lie a wide range of expectations for the future, of actions, solidarity, creative love, mysticism and politics.[16] This range in prophetic faith is common to the prophetic religions.

2. *Present freedom*

This basic experience gives rise to a specifically Christian emphasis. Christianity developed its identity at a time when there was a strong awareness of the present. It was an apocalyptic time, veering between despair and utopian hope, between the will to bring in a better future by force and a readiness to leave all the initiatives to God. The prophetic question had to be answered as to whether God is present here and now, as to whether the joy of the new beginning has already been given. Contrary to all appearances, Jesus says that the kingdom of God has already begun. This hidden beginning plays a great role in his parables. Now the lame can walk, the blind can see and prisoners can be freed (Luke 4.18f.). Now the Spirit of God which has been so long expected has been poured out over the small group (Acts 2.1–41). Now that all oppositions have been overcome (Gal. 3.28), we are freed for freedom (Gal. 5.1).

So in early Christianity, belief in Yahweh leads to an experience of freedom which breaks through existing barriers. The unconditional trust in God takes on a contemporary form; it becomes critical trust in self. Freedom becomes a divine power and the foundation for our future. The borderline between the human and the divine on the other side has become paper-thin, where it has not been obliterated altogether. Now transcendence and immanence have become usless concepts for describing the degree of the inwardness of God. We experience the God of our beyond when we drink here and now from our own wells.[17]

There is no question that with this experience of faith the Christian creed can also fit into inter-religious dialogue. Its revolutionary force has been rediscovered in our century and is also the cause of unrest within Christianity. The future, the kingdom of God, liberation, the reconciliation of men and women, of human beings and nature, a reversal of the power structures, belief in the breath of God in the present fight against the powers of death – all these images join together in the newly discovered experience that God is present in them. So trust in God becomes the inspired experience of freedom in us and in our history; it is none other than genuinely Christian belief in the Holy Spirit.[18] Perhaps one of the tasks of Christians is to guard this experience between past and future in the dialogue between the prophetic religions.

3. Historical identification

But when and how does this freedom become historical reality? The answer cannot be limited either topologically or chronologically, for in accordance with the biblical conviction the 'here and now' is all times and places in which human beings live. Only against this background is the foolhardy transition to the third dimension of faith understandable: it is faith in Jesus Christ. This dimension of faith is characterized not by trust or freedom in themselves, but by their involvement in an event. It is a matter of discipleship, of historical identification. Christians understand the history of Jesus of Nazareth as their messianic history. They stake everything on being able to measure their trust and their freedom by his history. Jesus becomes the decisive image, the decisive wisdom, the decisive word of God for them; in this dynamic sense, which has to be deciphered hermeneutically, God is active and at work in Jesus.[19]

This historical identification distinguishes Christian faith clearly from all other religions. The strength and danger of Christian faith lie in it. It produces clarity and vividness. God is reflected in a truly human image. Only those who discover the power of this elementary identification can also understand its high symbolization. The whole cosmos of biblical symbolism is now transferred to it. Jesus becomes the bearer of the Spirit, the 'Messiah', the 'Son of God', the divine, incarnate 'Word'. The danger of this symbolization is its exclusiveness and later its metaphysical, unhistorical, interpretation.

III Dimensions of the divine?

These observations were meant to sketch out three basic positions from which the multiplicity of Christian images of God developed. Christian faith grows out of a triadic impulse of trust, experience of freedom and discipleship. Shouldn't it be possible also to find such a triadic structure of Father, Son and Spirit in other religions? Probably it makes no sense to compare divine trinities schematically. What is of more help is the sober historical statement that only at a later stage did the New Testament and early Christian triad of Father, Son and Spirit become a triad within the Godhead and become associated with it.[20] Now there was no longer a description of the relationships between the Spirit or Jesus Christ and God, but a specification of relationships 'within the Godhead'. The 'external' Trinity of Father, Son and Spirit was grounded in a threeness within the deity.

This process is extremely interesting, since it brought to the centre dimensions of the divine which were easily suppressed in the image of the monotheistic (and at the same time monarchical and male) God, and which were urgently needed in the battle against contempt for the world, intolerance and an undemocratic world order.[21] If Christian faith is realized as trust, as an experience of freedom and discipleship, in other words if we encounter God not only in the beyond but also in ourselves and in history, then God cannot be grasped only in the image of the person in the beyond. Driven by this question, the Christian tradition has developed three basic symbols for God: the ineffable 'You', the Spirit and the Incarnate Word. Each of these three basic symbols offers a basic orientation for our talk of the divine; none of them can be dispensed with; only together do they form a framework which is appropriate protection for the mystery of the divine. It must be possible to introduce these basic symbols into inter-religious dialogue.

1. Spirit

We begin with the basic symbol 'spirit'. Spirit here is not understood in the a-materialistic sense of classical metaphysics, but as the breath of the divine which cannot be grasped and yet which enlivens all things, what John Hick calls the 'Inspirer'. It points to a basic religious experience which forms an intense bond between all religions: the divine of which we can only have an inkling, but which sinks into human hearts in all parts of this world and in the world as a whole. The presence of the breath of the divine is common to the past and the future. Religious people experience the presence of this holiness; they sink into it and thus encounter the limits of everything and nothing, of being and passing away.

Depending on the religious context, the interpretation of this spirit is broad and open. It speaks in the monotheistic traditions of communion and love. It extends from an ecstatic affirmation of this world to its consistent relativization, from a quest for present salvation to a quenching into nothingness. Anyone who enters into the ground of reality arrives at a comprehension which cannot be grasped. So 'Spirit' means the divine in its inexpressible nature, its presence and its absolute withdrawal.[22] Respect for this spirit leads to negative theologies, but also to a superfluity of discourse, since all the words in the world cannot grasp this experience.

2. *The ineffable 'You'*

Like 'Almighty', 'All-merciful' or 'Lord', 'Father' is only one of the possible symbols for the possibility of addressing a divine 'You'. This 'You' points to a basic dimension of the divine which has become a primary factor in the prophetic religions. Of course as soon as Jesus ceases to provide the context, the address 'Father' can become a restrictive and androcentric metaphor. But that is not the decisive factor. What is decisive, rather, is that here the divine is experienced as something over against, as an authority from the beyond, to which we can relate as persons, which knows us, accepts us and loves us.[23]

This second basic metaphor characterizes the prophetic religions: they all call on God in unconditional trust as the one Creator of heaven and earth. Whereas the immanent Spirit expresses itself as comprehensive present, this divine 'You' expresses itself as universal and transcendent oneness. So whereas the divine is immersed in the world, 'God' at the same time stands over the world. God confirms the world, since as an independent reality the world is distinct from God. In the face of the divine 'You' the all-important decisive answer is not silence but a thoughtful confession ('. . . with the heart and the lips', Rom. 10.9). Therefore the prophetic religions have always seen to it that God is addressed and spoken of.

God as the inexpressible 'You' stands for a controlled picture of the world, for the way from chaos to order, from oppression to justice, from the laborious journey to the final goal.[24] The interpretations of this basic movement, too, can be manifold and are to be included in the dialogue with the religions; for talk of 'God' and addressing God, questions of human freedom and the shaping of a human future, are not alien to them.[25] Love, forgiveness and unconditional affirmation also have everything to do with the divine.

3. *The incarnate Word*

The third basic metaphor is the most difficult to fit into inter-religious dialogue. It is 'incarnate Word' and means a God or a divine element which has entered into human history and taken human form. But in Christianity doesn't this mean Jesus of Nazareth? And mustn't this divine status of Jesus in particular lead to a contradiction of all other religions? Is it legitimate for a concrete historical person to enter into the basic symbolism of God and thus break through the distinction between God and human beings?

At this precise point everything depends on a distinction being made between the earliest Christian triadic impulses and the later doctrine of the Trinity.[26] Dialogue with other religions should not begin with the question of what Jesus Christ means for us Christians. It must begin with the question whether the 'divine' does not encounter us in a special way in certain historical figures. Can't it be the divine wisdom which according to biblical tradition dwells among us children of men (Prov. 8.22–31)? Can't it be God's Word which has taken the flesh of history in many places (John 1.1). Isn't it there in the historical concrete revelations which are also active in other religions?

So 'Word', 'Wisdom' and 'Revelation' denote those concrete memories (words, actions, writings) in which the divine can humble itself and assume an invisible form. The divine dwells among us in concrete histories, in victory and defeat. Each of these historically tangible histories is nothing in itself, is just a chance product of history. But at the same time it is possible for the divine to be given in them in a particular way; otherwise the divine cannot develop any historical force.

IV Threefold God – triune God?

So God and the divine can be seen and understood in three dimensions. God has sunk into the world and can be experienced as immediate presence. God stands over against the world and can be addressed as a personal 'You'. God takes constantly new form in human beings and their history. So the divine must be understood as 'You', as Spirit and as a history which has become concrete.

In the second part I spoke with restraint about a triad of Christian experience of God; in the third part about three dimensions which can be noted in God in any event. Fortunately the Christian doctrine of the Trinity has constantly stood as a warning to theology not to neglect any one of these three dimensions. The three dimensions are irreplaceable; each one takes up one aspect of the divine mystery. Now the traditional doctrine of the Trinity does not need correcting because it has reflected on these three dimensions and worked them out with the help of different models. It needs correction because it has fixed Christian faith in its concrete historical form on an unhistorical model.

That need not have happened; for the three dimensions of the divine, related to the one God, also produce a picture full of tensions, in themselves and independently of their christological application. The one God, as one and the same, is that which is over against me and is present in the depths of the world and in incarnate history. As Creator he was always there and will always be there; as Spirit he is at work in us; as the Word of history he goes with us into the future. So each time it is the one God, but never tangible, never fixed to one place or one dimension of time. All that we say of God is false, unless we add the other aspects as a corrective. So the threefold nature of God in turn becomes a paradoxical symbol. It is the symbol of ineffability and mystery in the strict sense of the word. With our language and thought we cannot penetrate deeper than to this penultimate level. The divine itself no longer has any names or words. It is hidden from us, in the beyond, in history. It no longer allows any decision between transcendence, immanence and historicity.

None of this is unknown to Christianity, but the Christian tradition was shaped by a quite different dynamic. The God of the Abrahamic religions has a name. He shows a way. This way became a clear historical figure in Christian faith. Christian identity cannot surrender this dynamic, for this God has nothing to do with flight from the world. He has a history, a future and a kingdom which begins here and now in human action. This, then, is a specific contribution of the Christian tradition. In it human beings become bearers of the divine mystery – in the utmost danger. Human beings become 'the story of God'.[27]

But what we Christians could learn again in dialogue with the other religions is this. In this action success and failure go together. Our great life history is and remains a history of passion. Therefore even the God of Abraham always remains a God whose true divinity ultimately escapes us. God is sacrament in that he gives himself to us. But he is also sacrament in that he conceals his divinity from us. In human history he shares what Thomas Aquinas calls his 'hidden deity' with us. So even active struggle for a just future can succeed only if it is accompanied by an ultimate passivity, a restrained approach to the divine.

Translated by John Bowden

Notes

1. Works on the history of the doctrine usually begin with statements by Justin and Irenaeus (second century). After the third century there are the great christological controversies which finally, after the fourth century, led to the development of the

doctrine of the Trinity. Cf. A. Grillmeier, *Christ in Christian Tradition*, Oxford
²1975; J. N. D. Kelly, *Early Christian Doctrines*, London 1958; G. W. H. Lampe,
God as Spirit, Oxford 1977; M. Wiles, 'Some Reflections on the Origins of the
Doctrine of the Trinity', in *Working Papers in Doctrine*, London 1976, 1–17.

2. H. Wipfler, *Grundfragen der Trinitätsspekulation*, Regensburg 1977. The best
account and analysis of the classical doctrine of the Trinity by a German author is to
be found in W. Pannenberg, *Systematic Theology* I, Grand Rapids and Edinburgh
1992, Chapter 5, 'The Trinitarian God'.

3. Unfortunately this problem has so far been concealed rather than clarified by
polemic within Christianity. One example of this is A. Dumas, 'Der einzige Gott,
Der Dreieinige Gott', in *Neue Summe Theologie* I, *Der Lebendige Gott*, Freiburg
1988, 426; cf. H. Häring, 'Wer is Gott, ausser unserem Gott?', in W. van Remmen,
Die Dreifaltigkeit Gottes im Leben des Christen, Kleve 1992, 149–67.

4. K. Rahner gave a classic account of this in one of his earliest articles, 'Theos in
the New Testament', *Theological Investigations* I, London and New York, 1961,
79–148.

5. C. Andresen. 'Antike und Christentum', *Theologische Realenzyklopädie* 3, 50–
98.

6. The first great trinitarian schemes of the Cappadocians (Basil of Caesarea,
Gregory of Nyssa, Gregory of Nazianzus) were produced in the East in the fourth and
fifth centuries; what they clarify and what they leave obscure is still a controlling
factor today.

7. R. Schreiter, *Constructing Local Theologies*, Maryknoll and London 1984.

8. K. Rahner, 'Remarks on the Dogmatic Treatise "De Trinitate"', in *Theological
Investigations* IV, New York and London 1966, 77–104.

9. L. Jacobs, *Principles of the Jewish Faith. An Analytical Study*, London 1964.

10. N. Smart, *The World's Religions. Old Traditions and Modern Transforma-
tions*, Cambridge 1989/1992; H. Smith, *The World's Religions*, New York 1991,
could serve as examples.

11. Unfortunately the controversial volume edited by J. Hick and P. F. Knitter,
The Myth of Christian Uniqueness, Maryknoll and London 1987, neglected this
aspect.

12. The trinitarian approaches in liberation theology, Black theologies and feminist
theology are analysed in E. Borgman, *Sporen van de bevrijdende God*, Kampen
1990; for the significance of praxis in inter-religious dialogue see Knitter, 'Towards a
Liberation Theology of Religions', in Hick and Knitter (eds.), *The Myth of Christian
Uniqueness* (n. 11), 178–200.

13. E. Schillebeeckx, *Christ*, London and New York 1980, gives an impression of
this wealth and creativity. Following Wittgenstein's theory of the language game,
christology should be deciphered in the light of these practical experiences.

14. D. Tracy, *The Analogical Imagination, Christian Theology and the Culture of
Pluralism*, London and New York 1981; J. Hick conjectures the triad 'Creator,
Redeemer, Inspirer', in 'The Non-Absoluteness of Christianity', in Hick and Knitter
(eds.), *The Myth of Christian Uniqueness* (n. 11), 16–36: 32.

15. K.-J. Kuschel, *Abraham. A Sign of Hope for Jews, Christians and Muslims*,
London and New York 1995.

16. J. W. Fowler, *Stages of Faith*, New York 1981; A. Schimmel, *Mystical
Dimensions of Islam*, Chapel Hill 1975.

17. G. Gutiérrez, *We Drink from our Own Wells. The Spiritual Journey of a People*, Maryknoll and London 1984; J. van Nieuwenhove, *Bronnen van bevrijding: Varianten in de theologie van Gustavo Gutiérrez*, Kampen 1991; see also Y. Congar, *I Believe in the Holy Spirit*, London 1983; M. A. Chevalier, *Souffle de Dieu, Le Saint-Esprit dans le Nouveau Testament* I–III, Paris 1972–91.

18. Borgman, *Sporen van de bevrijdende God* (n. 12), 202–81.

19. Since his fundamental work *On Being a Christian*, London and New York 1977, Hans Küng has been concerned with this hermeneutical decipherment in terms of categories of action; cf. also *Does God Exist?*, London 1984; *Judaism*, London and New York 1993; *Christianity, Essence and History*, London and New York 1995.

20. This process still remains comprehensible in Eastern theology, since there the uniqueness and pre-eminence of the Father remain undisputed. But it takes on a new quality in Augustine, since following the Neo-Platonist Marius Victorinus he transferred the human psychology of his time (the theory of remembering, knowing and willing) to God and in so doing shaped Western theology. Only now did a triangular model develop, according to which the three divine persons always acted at the same time and issued into one another as memory, knowing and willing. This process is repeated in Thomas Aquinas, who supported the Christian triad with a theory of subsisting relationships (for a summary see Küng, *Christianity*, n. 19).

21. J. Moltmann, *The Trinity and the Kingdom of God*, London and New York 1971; Dumas, 'Der einzige Gott' (n. 3), 415–17; M. de Dieguez, *L'idole monothéiste*, Paris 1981; A. de Benoist, *Comment peut-on être paien?*, Paris 1981.

22. E. Jüngel, *God as the Mystery of the World*, Grand Rapids and Edinburgh 1983.

23. H. Küng, *Does God Exist?* (n. 20), G II.

24. J. B. Metz, '"Time without a Finale": The Background to the Debate on "Resurrection or Reincarnation"', *Concilium* 1993/5, 124–31.

25. H. Küng, *Global Responsibility*, London and New York 1991.

26. For understandable reasons, since Rahner it has been pointed out that the 'economic' and the 'immanent' Trinity may not be separated. This has involuntarily led to a re-Hellenizing of the problem. Because of this it is therefore necessary to insist that the two should be strictly divided, if not separated. Anyone who calls for this is not repudiating the confession of the threefold God but taking account of the asymmetry which has arisen as a result of the confrontation of biblical and Hellenistic thought.

27. E. Schillebeeckx, *Church. The Human Story of God*, London and New York 1990; Jüngel, *God as the Mystery of the World* (n. 22), 409–543 (On the humanity of God).

II · Dimensions of Religious Experience of God

God in Ntomba Prayer

Laurent Mpongo

At minor seminary, I learned that prayer is 'the lifting up of the soul to God'. Subsequently, a work of Tauler's taught me that prayer is the 'lifting up of the heart to God'. All that was very disconcerting. Referring to the religion of my Ntomba ancestors, I noted that prayer is a corporate word which a person or a human group addresses either to ancestors or to God. Through this corporate word it is possible to grasp the name which the Ntomba give to the Supreme Being and the images which they form of this Being.

In this article I shall first introduce the divine name which recurs a great deal in Ntomba prayer. Then we shall look at some representations of God among the Ntomba.[1] We shall end by recognizing that the God invoked by the Ntomba is the true God.

I A very usual divine name

In everyday life, in oaths, bets, animated conversations, vows, disputes, the Ntomba call to witness the Supreme Being under the name 'Nzambe'. The word Nzambe is also used by numerous African ethnic groups and can be found in a geographical area which extends from the Ivory Coast to Botswana.[2]

Nzambe comes from the root Nyam, which means 'shine'. So Nzambe denotes a luminous being on whom humans cannot fix their gaze. Shining and covered all over with the mantle of his brightness, Nzambe resides up there, above people's heads, in the firmament. He is said to be a 'heavenly' being. Thus the Ntomba recognize that God is transcendent, majestic, powerful. That is why the Ntomba and other Bantu groups call Nzambe to witness. To do that they make a sign with the index finger of the right hand which they draw across their heads. Then they raise the finger to heaven and cry 'Nzambe'. To cry 'Nzambe' at a moment of crisis is to hand oneself over to the one who, up there in the heavens, sees and knows all that is going on among mortals in the region below.

The missionaries who analysed the circumstances in which the Ntomba say 'Nzambe' understood that this people knew the God to whom they themselves prayed. For them 'Nzambe' was equivalent to the French word 'Dieu', 'God'.

According to the anthropology of religion, 'God' is a generic term denoting powers which do not fall into the category of beings of terrestrial origin, human beings. Among the Ntomba and other groups from the same linguistic area, Nzambe denotes a personal being. Moreover, as a name Nzambe puts the being who bears it in a relationship of dialogue with those who mention or call on the name. This relationship of dialogue attests that the name God given to a person and being who is powerful and transcendent expresses the living experience of human beings rather than the philosophical preoccupations of a school. Thus the name God/Nzambe is the object of religious rather than philosophical discourse.

From the Ntomba's religious experience of the God whom they name in their prayers, we can focus on their representations of God.

II The representations of God

A luminous being, Nzambe presents himself as 'the sun on which human beings cannot fix their gaze'.[3] This metaphor expresses the transcendence of God, God's power and knowledge. It leads the Ntomba to trust themselves to Nzambe at all times, even more when they become aware that they are incapable of coping with situations in life which are beyond them. The Ntomba raise their eyes to Nzambe, seeing themselves as plaintiffs pleading their cause. From this perspective, the Ntomba are inspired by the cultural meaning of the word *samba*[4] and form the verb *sambela* (pray). This verb is used when the Ntomba address Nzambe for the needs of their own cause. They use the verb *sambelela* (pray for) when they address God on behalf of someone else.

1. Supported by the world beyond

The missionaries who evangelized the Ntomba noticed that the word verb *sambela* was equivalent to their verb 'pray'. Good linguists, from the root *samb* they formed the noun *losambo* as a synonym for the term 'prayer'. Immediately, going by the cultural significance of the verb *samba*, the Ntomba thought that *losambo*/prayer in fact meant the presentation of one's grievances, requests, to Nzambe, the all-powerful being.

There are several kinds of prayers (*nsambo*) among the Ntomba, as there are among other Bantu peoples. The variety of prayers[5] is a function of the feelings of the individual or a human group about its human condition. There are both customary prayers, and occasional prayers or prayers in particular circumstances.

Customary prayers are those which accompany the actions of everyday life. These prayers find their *raison d'être* in the view of the world common to Black Africans. According to this view, the world comes to life and breathes to the degree that it is supported by the world beyond. In this context, all the human activities which form the framework of everyday life have to be performed before the face of, and under the protection of, the ancestors and Nzambe/God. Thus when he visits his nets, the Ntomba fisherman pauses for a moment before drawing the first net from the water. He will say, for example, 'Ngoya mpao' ('I have come to fish'). 'Nko Bomèlè' ('It all depends on the Owner').

2. *God – the Owner*

Nzambe/God is Bomèlè, the Owner. Everything belongs to him. The fisherman has to be aware of this. So fishing is an activity which signifies the generosity of Nzambe, the owner of the fish. A fisherman who did not think like this would, rightly, be accounted a thief.

Occasional prayers, or prayers in special circumstances, are those which are said at any time when individuals or human groups want to reinforce their vital force or to protect their lives from threat. To see how this happens, we might consider a ceremony which illustrates the nature of an occasional prayer. Even in our time the Ntomba think that Tuesday is the day when the dead come out of their abodes for nourishment. On that day living beings cannot go to the fields, to fish or to hunt outside the village, since they would run the risk of coming upon a dead person. That would mean certain death. So they have to stay in the village and perform a rite to protect themselves against the baneful influence of the dead. Thus down to the 1960s, in rural areas, the chief of the clan would gather his people in his enclosure and perform a prophylactic rite. Sitting on a stool, he would take white kaolin and use it to draw a line on each of his arms from shoulder to fist. Then he would get up and say in a loud voice:

We have no dispute
with the Owner of the earth;

We have no dispute
with the Maker of things
visible and invisible;
We have no dispute
with the Owner of breath.[6]

This profession of faith by the chief of the clan describes several typical features of Nzambe. During the prophylactic Tuesday rite God is not called Nzambe. He is called 'Owner of the earth' (*'Momb'iwanda'*), 'Maker of things visible and invisible' (*'Wang'ilonga'*), and finally 'Owner of breath, of life' (*Mom'ikopi'*).

These representations of God lead the Ntomba to think that God is *Ntedni* (judge), or the one who settles disputes authoritatively.

3. God – judge

The idea that God is judge stems from the fact that the verb *sambela* ('pray') culturally evokes a legal context. Individuals or the group pray to Nzambe because they see him as one who transcends all things and who can therefore settle disputes in an impartial way. That is why the staunch Ntomba will say that God 'does not sleep'. At the due moment he will render justice to the one on trial. Then God is Nkumu, chief, the one of note, since he governs all. He reigns. This term Nkuma is used in catechesis and the Christian liturgy.

Finally, the Nzambe invoked by the Ntomba is not a mythological God. He is the true God.

III Nzambe, the true God

The Nzambe whom the Ntomba and other Bantu people invoke is not a mythological God. He is a personal being. The Ntomba also call on Nka Miônga, the Ancestor Majesty of the Ancestors. All human beings bow before Nka Miônga, saying 'Majesty' (Miônga), while clapping their hands. The Ntomba represent Nka Miônga as a chief with crown and medals, sitting on a throne. Such a chief has no equal. He is worthy of respect and praise. Before him human beings confess how small and unworthy they are. They lower their heads and cannot look at him.

The title Nka Miônga given to Momb'iwanda, the Maker of things visible and invisible, impressed the missionaries. They used it in the act of contrition, which begins with the words 'Nka Miônga, momb'iwanda enkimi'.[7]

1. The only God

Given the adage *lex orandi, lex credendi*, despite its origins, we recognize that the liturgical usage of terms like Nzambe, Momb'iwanda, Nka Miônga and Nkumu allows us to think that the God called on under these names before the arrival of the missionaries is the true God. He is the God who also manifested himself to Moses on Horeb, calling himself '*Ehyeh asher ehyeh*', 'He who is there as he is there'. So it is unnecessary to revive the controversies which once divided schools of ethnology over whether or not the primitive peoples of Africa, for example, professed monotheism. The God invoked by the Black Africans is the one God whom the Mosaic and Christian revelation also presents as creator of heaven and earth, and just as the Holy Spirit 'is already at work before the glorification of Christ',[8] so we believe that this one God revealed himself to the Bantu ancestors by the Holy Spirit, 'the one who does not speak in a loud voice but murmurs constantly a discourse on the trinitarian God'.[9]

2. The God of traditional religion

At a time when 'inculturation' or, better, the dialogue between Christianity in its Western form and the non-Christian religions is the fashion, it is necessary to consider the evidence. We must take seriously a profession of faith made by John Paul II: 'All authentic prayer is prompted by the Holy Spirit, who is mysteriously present in the human heart'.[10]

The recognition of the presence of the Spirit of God in the human heart leads me to share the following conviction: 'In short, Christianity in its Western form as it has been presented by the missionaries does not replace traditional religion . . . It simply plays the role of the yeast in the dough, which in this case is traditional religion. Thanks to this yeast, that is, Christianity in its Western form, traditional religion is being regenerated in an awareness that it must have a christological dimension.'[11]

That is why the task of the Christianity which has reached the Africans in a Western form is to help traditional religion to discover that the Spirit and the Incarnate Word are, according to the saying of Irenaeus of Lyons, the 'two hands' by which the Father moulds it, so that it can understand that the God whom it has always confessed and invoked is in reality the trinitarian God revealed by Jesus Christ.

IV Conclusion

This article has shown that dogmatic theology functions well only when it is done in good conditions. Among these, one has to include popular modes of appropriating the religious values or the religious experiences of a people.

The evocation of the religious experiences of the Ntomba from attitudes reflected in some of their prayers has enriched our religious vocabulary about God. It has also introduced us to the representations of God among the Ntomba. Furthermore, it has nurtured a profound conviction in us: *the God of the Ntomba is the true God known also by the Jews*. The evangelizing action of the church must mould traditional religion so that it unfolds its christological dimension under the action of the Holy Spirit.

Translated by John Bowden

Notes

1. I am speaking of the Ntomba who live in the Inongo region of Bandundu.
2. This word has several variants: Zamba, Nyame, Nsambe, Nzambi, Anzambe, etc.
3. This metaphor is used in the eucharistic prayer of what is currently called the 'Zairean Rite for the Celebration of the Eucharist'.
4. *Samba* means to plead a cause, negotiate for an agreement.
5. *Losambo* (plural *nasambo*). *Nsambo* can also denote dances. It confirms that 'prayer' is a corporate word.
6. '*Yêlo, nko Momb'iwanda; Yêlo, nko Wang'ilonga; Yêlo, nko Mom'ikopi*', cf. N. van Everbroeck, *Momb'ipoku*, Tervuren 1961, 58.
7. 'Ancestor Majesty of the Ancestors, for me you are the Owner of the earth.'
8. John Paul II, *Redemptoris missio*, no. 29.
9. L. Mpongo, *Le colloque de Aachen. Les souvenirs d'un Africain* (manuscript), 3.
10. *AAS* 79, 1987, 1087.
11. Mpongo, *Colloque* (n. 9), 4.

The Experience of God in Jesus Christ

Bruno Forte

'It began with an encounter. Some people . . . came into contact with Jesus of Nazareth and stayed with him . . . This astonishing and overwhelming encounter with the man Jesus became the starting point for the New Testament view of salvation. To put it plainly, "grace" has to be expressed in terms of encounter and experience; it can never be isolated from the specific encounter which brought about liberation.'[1] For Christian faith, salvation comes about in this human experience of divine self-communication which the encounter with the living Lord, the Holy Spirit, made possible at the beginnings of the Christian movement in history and continues to make possible – albeit in different forms – at all times: the experience of God in Jesus Christ. The encounter is not simply the fruit of an inner openness on the part of the human being, something that 'comes about' in men and women by virtue of their potentialities; nor is it the result of a transcendent divine action which eliminates or ignores the active reception of the creature, something which 'happens' to people without any free contribution on their part.

The encounter is a covenant celebration, initiated by God with human beings, and matched – though in an asymmetrical way – by an active human response to the living God. The Christian experience of salvation thus has two inseparable aspects: on the one hand it is the authentic human experience of divine self-communication, and on the other it is a sacramental event, a fragment of history in which the divine comes to dwell and to communicate itself to human beings.

I The human experience of divine self-communication

To speak of the human experience of divine self-communication is not to reduce the supernatural to the co-ordinates of the 'penultimate' world; this language simply seeks to express the law of the 'economy' of salvation, through which the living God communicates himself to human beings in ways which are practical for them, in order to establish real contact with them. The divine condescension as such is that the invisible offers itself in the visible, the infinite in the finite, and eternity in the concrete determinations and limitations of time, though without the transcendence being dissolved into immanence. There is a surplus in revelation which remains hidden, so that whatever of the divine is made accessible presents itself as a revelation which is also a concealing.

1. Experience – etymology

What does it mean that human beings – thanks to the event of revelation – have 'experience' of divine self-communication? Etymology helps to clarify the concept of 'experience': made up of '*ex*' and '*perior*', the Latin word *experientia* on the one hand evokes an exodus, a 'going out from' and a 'going towards', and on the other – through the use of the verb *perior*, which appears only in composite terms – denotes the two fields of meaning connected with this word. The verb underlies both *peritus* and *periculum*: the *peritus* is the one who has an immediate and direct knowledge of things; *periculum* denotes the risk, the test, the imponderable element connected with any direct contact (in just the same way the Greek *peira* denotes 'test, risk, attempt, experiment', and the verb *peiro* means 'moving from one place to another', 'crossing, traversing, navigating': the word 'port' is connected with the same etymology). Experience is 'travelling through the country' (like the original meaning of the German *erfahren* = experiment, meaning '*Land fahren*' = crossing the country), risking the unknown, characterized by the immediacy of vision and knowledge.

So the knowing in experience is concrete and immediate, not based on hearsay but on personal contact, and involving the whole of the protagonist, both senses and intellect. It implies a risk and calls for boldness, stimulating the person to be alive and active towards what is happening (the German *erleben*, another term for denoting experience, means 'being alive to the event'). So experience involves not only the existential level of the person, determining or modifying his or her way of seeing life, but also the 'existentive level', the relationship to the complex of events in which the experience is situated.

2. Risen from the dead

How are these characteristics of human experience realized in the encounter with the divine self-communication in Jesus Christ? Here, too, there is an immediacy which takes place in the 'fullness' of time in the personal encounter with the historical Jesus and the One risen from the dead; it continues by means of the witnesses and the Word of life which they proclaim (cf. Rom. 10.14f.). Here too there is a risk: the test is that through the visible and the audible the human protagonists in the encounter are called on to become open to the invisible and to silence, in order to recognize that here the Lord is showing himself alive. And this happens in the free and risky decision of giving oneself to the God who reveals himself and in the act of unconditional turning towards this God.

It is the stories of the 'appearances of the risen Lord' which allow us to reconstruct the characteristics of the human experience of the divine self-communication, realized in encounter with the Risen Lord. The five groups of narratives (I Cor. 15.5–8; Mark 16.9–20; Matt. 28.9–10, 16–20; Luke 14.13–53; John 20.14–29; 21) cannot be harmonized in accordance with a complete and coherent scheme based on chronological and geographical details; moreover, such a material harmonization is outside the interests of the New Testament writings, which are a testimony of faith based on history, and certainly not a chronicle of 'plain facts'. However, it is possible to discover in the various accounts of the appearances a structure which keeps returning, marked by three basic elements. The initiative of the Risen Christ is followed by a process on the part of the disciples of recognizing Jesus of Nazareth in the one who presents himself alive; mission draws on this encounter – charged with 'objective' and 'subjective' elements – as an expression of the transforming experience which has been lived through.

It is the Risen Christ who takes the initiative in the accounts of the appearances: 'He presented himself to them alive' (Acts 1.3). He appears in person: although the verb *ophthe* used in I Cor. 15.3–8 and Luke 24.34 (cf. Acts 9.17; 13.31; 26.16) is susceptible to a passive interpretation, 'was seen', 'was made (by God) to be seen', or, in the middle, can mean 'made to appear', 'appeared', it is used in the Greek Old Testament to describe theophanies (cf. Gen. 12.7; 17.1; 18.1; 26.2). So it is the initiative of the Lord which is emphasized: it is he who shows himself alive, appears and speaks. This visual and auditory experience is not something which 'comes into being' in those to which it is addressed, but is something that 'happens' to them, and comes from outside; in other words, it is an objective, distinct, external experience. The 'vision', like the subjective experience of seeing, does not have pride of place in the stories; that is held by the fact that the Risen Christ 'showed himself alive'. The Risen Christ is seen because he 'appears'; he does not appear because he 'is seen'. In this marked emphasis on the objectivity of the human experience of revelation the Easter stories are in perfect continuity with Old Testament faith: it is the living God who takes the initiative in communicating himself to human beings, in the utmost freedom and gratuitousness.

What marks out the completion of the preparation is that now the Word offers himself in his flesh: here is the Word become human, that Jesus who had been crucified and who now shows himself risen from the dead. The 'seeing' now plays a greater role than in the Old Covenant, precisely because 'the Word was made flesh . . . and we have seen his glory' (John 1.14); however, the 'word' remains determinative, because the appearance of the Risen Christ usually culminates in a saying about calling, memory or mission. Above all, however, seeing and hearing are united in the initiative manifestly taken by the one who appears and speaks. Here is the continuity with the Old Testament revelation and at the same time the scandalous newness: that God makes himself present and speaks in Jesus Christ, the eternal Word who has entered into history.

3. Recognition

The initiative of the risen Christ is followed by recognition on the part of those to whom he appears: this is a process of reaction and response which comes about through amazement and doubt, overcome through a word or an action of the Lord (cf. Luke 24.30f., 35, 37, 49–43; John 20.14, 16, 20; 21.4, 6f.; cf. Matt. 28.7) and resolved in the joyful confession, 'It is the Lord'. This gradual process is evidence of the gratuitousness and freedom of the assent which the disciples are called to give: the one who appears does not compel, but offers himself and appeals for the generous self-surrender of recognition in faith and love. The difficulty in the 'surrender' for those to whom Christ appears lies in the surprising 'newness' of the form in which the Risen Christ presents himself: he is the Living One who radiates fullness of life and is not bound by the fetters of finitude (cf. John 20.19; Luke 24.31). This newness does not eliminate the continuity with the past, though at the height of the process 'their eyes were opened and they recognized him' (Luke 24.31). The response of those to whom Christ appears is expressed not only by their confessions of faith (cf. e.g. John 20.28, 'My Lord and my God') but also by the urgent need that they feel to repeat the word which has reached them through missionary action: thus the disciples of the Emmaus road, having recognized Jesus in the breaking of the bread, 'left without delay and returned to Jerusalem . . . and reported what had happened . . .' (Luke 24.33, 35).

Here, too, the continuity with the Old Testament experience of revelation emerges: the prophet, reached and indwelt by the Word, repeats it, proclaims it with all his life. Here, too, the newness of the fulfilment lies wholly in the reference to the person of Christ: the recognition and confession of him, expressed in the joyful certainty that 'It is the Lord' (John 21.7). The human experience of God's self-communication is now wholly realized in the encounter with the Lord Jesus; it is to him in person that the wonder of adoration and the assent of faith is expressed: he is the object of the proclamation and the foundation of the hope which changes life.

4. Mission

The new beginning in the life of the disciples, mission, derives from their encounter with the Risen Christ, whom they recognize and welcome: the fearful fugitives of Good Friday become the courageous witnesses to Easter. The encounter has transformed them: the 'objectivity' of the Lord's initiative recognized through the 'subjective' itinerary of faith and love has changed their existence, making them transparent and contagious proclaimers of the one whom they have experienced (cf. Matt. 28.18–20; Luke 24.48; John 20.19ff.). Now they can affirm: 'God has raised him from the dead and of this we are witnesses' (Acts 3.15; cf. Acts 2.32; 5.31; 10.40f.). Paul wants to see himself as part of this current of radiant testimony: 'For I delivered to you as of first importance what I also received, that Christ died for our sins according to the scriptures, that he was buried, that he was raised on the third day in accordance with the scriptures, and that he appeared to Cephas, then to the twelve' (I Cor. 15.3–5).

Here the incarnate Word who has shown himself alive in the Easter experience of the appearances reveals himself to full effect: this revelation really transforms the life of those whom he reaches, changes and renews history, awakens unforeseen energy, gives vigour and passion to the witnesses. On this point, too, there is marked continuity with the Old Testament experience of revelation in which the word does what it says, creating and recreating the world and life.

And here, too, the newness of the fulfilment emerges: Christ the Word made flesh, the power of the gospel, the effective force in testimony, corroborating it with his Holy Spirit. And in Christ it is the access to the mystery of the Father which now renews hearts and history: 'If a man loves me, he will keep my word, and my Father will love him, and we will come to him and make our home with him' (John 14.23). The mission is to extend to the whole world that of which the witnesses have experience: him and the power of the resurrection in him (cf. Phil. 3.10).

5. The singularity of Jesus Christ

So a comparison of the Old Testament experience of revelation with the fullness of time constituted by the Easter events shows the profound continuity and unity of the experience of God in the Judaeo-Christian tradition: the initiative of the Lord and the response of human beings, the coming and the exodus, constitute the two co-ordinates (asymmetrical because of the surplus of grace) from which the new element which the revelation transmits and brings about in the history of the world derives. The newness of the fulfilment consists in the fact that all this is now uniquely and definitively realized in Jesus Christ: the 'singularity' of the Crucified and Risen One is the true element of absoluteness in Christianity, the fullness which surpasses all preparation and waiting.

This 'singularity' means that in him alone does the divine advent fully take place, because he is God's personal self-communication, the Son who reveals the Father in the Holy Spirit; it also means that in him this divine advent has assumed and made its own the exodus of the human condition, in such a way that nothing human can now be kept separate or apart from the love of God. Jesus the Christ is in person the encounter with the advent and the exodus of the divine coming and the human going, the concrete and personal universal in which the divine truth 'destines' itself to provide the basis for the unity of the 'already' and the 'not yet', on which every story of finite freedom and hope is constructed and in which it is situated.

II The experience of God in the sacramental event

1. Christ – the great sacrament

According to the great Christian tradition, the place in which the self-communication of God approaches human experience in time is the sacramental event in which the divine advent offers itself to be seen and heard, to be touched and tasted by the human senses in a more fitting way. The 'mystery-sacrament' is the making present of the salvific action of the transcendent God through the mediation of words and actions in this world, which the Spirit uses as instruments of the divine self-communication: it is the glory which comes to hide itself and at the same time to shine out in the signs of history.

In this light, the great sacrament of God is Christ, the Word made flesh, the Word coming forth from the Silence to pitch its tent in our midst. This Word is visible Word: 'For this is the will of my Father, that every one who sees the Son and believes in him should have eternal life; and I will raise him up at the last day' (John 6.40). It is audible: 'He who hears my word and believes him who sent me has eternal life' (John 5.24). It is tangible: 'Put your finger here, and see my hands, and put out your hand, and place it in my side; do not be faithless, but believing' (John 20.27). It can be tasted: 'He who eats my flesh and drinks my blood abides in me and I in him' (John 6.54). Jesus is the supreme self-communication of God, the eternal Son who has come among us, Emmanuel.

2. The church

From testimony to testimony, in the power of the Spirit, the direct contact with the living Christ is handed down in time, in such a way that faith in him is not based on what is said, but on the experience that the living can have of him in the Word and in the Spirit. Here there emerges the fundamental role of the transmission of the apostolic faith in the church, the concrete historical place where Christ can be experienced. In such a way, the senses – which are so evocative in human experience – are fully involved in the actual encounter with revelation: 'The senses are that part of the soul which is externalized and Christ is God who has externalized himself.'[2] So the senses and Christ are made to encounter each other, and this happens in the church: 'Christ appears to the individual in the global image of the church, in the community of faith which is always alive and lives in history. The church is the narrowest scope of the radiation of his form. His ray not only falls on it, as on the images of the world, but penetrates it so that it can be actively resplendent in return.'[3]

So, participating in the original sacramentality of Christ, the church is itself in time a sacrament of salvation, a concrete form, historically determined, of participation in the divine life in human time, the 'body of Christ', 'temple of the Spirit', 'icon of the Trinity'. In this sense the church is the living historical mediation of revelation, the making present of the Word and the silence of God to human existence in the power of the Spirit. It is the mystery of the encounter in its communal and social form, the people created by the Word to adore the Silence and to bring back to their Origin the dispersed sons and daughters of God in the power of the Comforter.

The divine gift in the economy of the words and signs willed by the Lord is handed down in the church; in it the understanding of the revealed truth is developed under the guidance of the Spirit, and the interpretation of the message and its vital communication to the human heart, the experience of God in Jesus Christ, is made possible in a truer way.

3. The sacraments

The sacrament which is the church finds the culmination and source of its own experience in the specific events of the sacraments: the sacraments are the events of the divine self-communication, offered according to the economy of the needs of the birth, growth and healing of redeemed existence, in its personal and ecclesial aspects. In it the revelation of the mystery is actualized through the action of the Holy Spirit, the transcendent agent necessary for all sacramental acts: the Word is made present and contagious in its economy of incarnation, and at the same time the Silence – revealing itself as the ultimate and hidden Origin – makes itself accessible as a goal and a home.

In this sense the sacrament embraces the economy of the Word: far from being separate, Word and sacramental event are part of the one dispensation in time of the gift of the divine self-communication, completed in revelation. The Word resounds as an 'audible sacrament' and the sacrament is offered as a 'visible word', the maximum concentration of the revelatory event which is the Word of God. Truly, *accedit verbum et fit sacramentum*: the sacrament is the event of the Word in its full completeness!

III Word, Silence and Encounter

So in the sacramental act the whole economy of revelation is made present and accessible: Word, Silence and Encounter are brought together in the sober concreteness of the sign, to be communicated in it, but without being exhausted in it. In the grace of the sacramental Encounter, the work of the Spirit, resounds the Word proceeding from the Silence and reaching the human heart to communicate to it the divine life; in this very grace, through the Word, the creature listens to the silence and prepares to celebrate the glory with the whole of its existence. The gift of revelation comes from the Father through the Son in the Spirit, so that in the Spirit through the Son everything returns to the Father, and 'God is all in all' (cf. I Cor. 15.28).

From the Silence through the Word in the communion of encounter is communicated the divine life in the sacramental events, so that in the personal and ecclesial experience of the encounter, by listening to and following the Word, there is celebrated in every heart the glory of the Origin, and the whole universe is orientated on and moves towards the Silence which is its home. A careful inter-religious dialogue cannot but ask how this interplay of Word, Silence and Encounter comes about in other human experiences of the divine; to have examined these basic elements in the experience of God in Jesus Christ is a precondition of faithfulness to one's own identity, thanks to which such a dialogue becomes possible and fruitful for Christians.

Translated by John Bowden

Notes

1. E. Schillebeeckx, *Christ*, London and New York 1980, 19.
2. Hans Urs von Balthasar, *Glory, I. Seeing the Form*, Edinburgh 1983, 376.
3. Ibid., 388.

Meister Eckhart: The Postponement of Unity as a Sphere of Life

Frans Maas

Eckhart's mysticism is steeped in a Neoplatonic fascination with unity. As a result it seems a priori by no means obvious that we should investigate a contemporary theme like the 'many faces of the divine' through this figure of the late Middle Ages. But here appearances are deceptive. I shall show that for Eckhart unity is constantly postponed. This makes space for different forms of religious life and for the many faces of God. In the adjournment of unity, diversity takes on a dynamic and a perspective.

To begin with, I shall briefly outline Eckhart's way of thinking, distinguishing three elements of his mystical rhythm: absence, the birth of God and the breakthrough into the Godhead. Then I shall demonstrate the postponement of unity in each of these three elements.

I A trinitarian rhythm of mysticism

If we are to follow Eckhart's theological argument we must begin from the Neoplatonic intuition of an original and ultimate unity of all things. Plurality is simply a derivative. This unity is life; otherwise there is no life. That life is God. Resting in itself, it is at the same time absolute superfluity. It wells up in an outgoing movement which at the same time remains within – thus one of his many paradoxes. In a trinitarian interpretation: the Father gives birth to the Son as equal to himself. And the 'returning', ingoing movement of love is essentially the same as the outgoing love of giving birth: the Son is constantly made one with the Father, and that is the Spirit. This stream of trinitarian life is an image of the superfluity of the One who is Hidden.

Now it is typical that for Eckhart in principle (i.e. as the primal image of all things) the whole creation is already given in this trinitarian stream: the whole outgoing possibility of creation lies within the Son. Eckhart calls this identity of primal images of creatures with the one image (the Son) the first bringing forth. The life of the Trinity is 'afterwards' (the quotation-marks indicate that this word does not have a temporal significance) active as God the creator. The outgoing movement is extended further in a 'second' moment of creation. This is creation in the usual sense, and here the threefold causality comes into play.[1]

The Father brings forth the creation in time and space, as something other than himself. This is the splintering into plurality which Eckhart usually calls creatureliness. It is a fall from the One; it is particularity, and thus – from the perspective of the one perfection – really nothing. But in practical pastoral care it emerges time and again that people want to hold on to this creaturely fragmentation, in countless forms of security. Eckhart's plea for detachment calls for an abandonment of this kind of self-preservation. He goes a long way in this: not to persist in the fragmentation of creation also means bidding farewell to God-as-creator, i.e. the Father who is the causal force which brings the external creation into being, as something other than himself.

However, this Father works outwardly in accordance with the primal images brought forth in the first outcoming. These are one in the Son. This exemplary causality means that the creation is essentially formed in the likeness of the Son. Therefore there is nothing other than God at the foundation of creation, however much he is also there in the fragmentation of time and space. Those who bid farewell to this dispersion come to the ground which they also have in creation, where God brings forth his eternally-begotten Son, as permanent divine life. As 'Lebemeister', Eckhart speaks here of the birth of God in the soul. In this form human beings are also essentially one with God and all creatures, in the primal image.

The Creator Spirit is the force behind the returning, inward movement in the Father. As the purposive cause the Spirit guides what was outside – although in the Son it is still one and within – back into the One who is Hidden, beyond the Father as creator and cause of the outgoing. This is the theme of the 'breakthrough into the Godhead' – the final goal. Here it emerges that human beings – this is in fact said only of human beings – on their way through creation still had more original unity than the created unity of the causal form: they had 'something' ('something in the soul') of the One who is Hidden in himself, unity even 'before' (not temporal, in the sense of more original), as the one primal image already stands in relationship to the multiplicity. For our imaginative capacity this is a unity which still lies 'behind' God as trinitarian life, the *Deus absconditus*. This is the theme of the 'nobility' or the 'citadel' of the soul which appears in the sermons.

To sum up: God's one overflowing life (the Father) streams over into new life (the Son). Here it is not lost, but streams outside, in a breakthrough, into the innermost being of God (the Spirit). Eckhart can only interpret this image of God as the one overflowing life in trinitarian terms. In human life the three elements correspond to a threefold postponement of the unity.

II Absence

As creator, God propels outwards, on the way. As creation the world is no longer a unity; it is simply something particular. But human beings have a tendency to cling on to this particularity; they want to make it an identity, to give themselves a settled home. However, the true person is on the way.

1. Being on the way

'The one who is on the way and is constantly on the way . . . he is the heavenly man. This means that you have no end and are never finished and never have anywhere to stand' (Q 188f., M 57f.).

People want to be as much at home as possible, to have arrived within a coherent whole that they can grasp. For religious people, God often functions as the focal point of this premature wholeness. But human beings have to bid farewell to this tendency towards premature oneness and to corresponding images of God: that is detachment.

So God is sometimes a function of human well-being.

'But many people want to look on God as they look on a cow, and they want to love God as they love a cow. You love it for its milk and cheese and all that it can give you. This is what all those people do who love God for outward riches and inward comfort: however, they do not love God, but their own interest' (Q 227, M 67).

Another way of coping which must be abandoned is bargaining with God. One can see this particularly with virtuous people who turn their faith into a work. Eckhart preaches on the gospel about the cleansing of the temple:

'Look, all those are merchants who are on their guard against gross sins and who want to do their works for God's honour, like fasting, keeping vigils, praying and suchlike; there are all kinds of good works, but they do them so that our Lord will do something for them in return, or give them something that they want: these are all merchants' (Q 153, M 31f.).

Sometimes even 'doing God's will' can give the illusion of a religious identity. In that case a person derives from it a self-satisfaction which cripples religious growth. Moreover, preaching on poverty of the spirit, Eckhart reacts fiercely to this holy little home. Those who seek steadfastly to practise what they see as God's will not have understood anything about it:

'If one of you should now ask me what it is, a poor man who does not "want anything", then my reply is as follows: as long as someone still insists that it is his "will" to fulfil the dearest will of God, he does not have the poverty of which we are speaking . . . As long as you have the will to fulfil the will of God and have a desire for eternity and for God, you are not poor' (Q 304, M 95).

2. *The nameless God*

Conceptual coherence, too, is simply transitory and must be broken up. Even the unity of the most venerable theology is transitory and must yield through a negative movement.

'God is not being nor goodness. God is not good nor better nor the best. Anyone who says God is good does him as much of an injustice as if one were to call the sun black' (Q 197). 'If he is not goodness, truth nor unity, what is he, then? He is sheer nothingness, he is still that' (DW I, 402). 'God is nameless, for no one can predicate or know anything of him. Therefore a pagan master says: what we know or say of the first source goes beyond what that first cause would be, since this is above any expression and understanding. So if I say, "God is good", that is not true; rather, I am good, but God is not good! . . . So Augustine says: the best that a man can say about God is to keep silent here out of the wisdom of inner riches' (Q 353, M 109).

Names for God function well only when they not only give orientation but also retreat to make room for ultimate unity, though this can only be attained by postponement, i.e. negatively. The many names of God are best in their reticence.

III The birth of God in the soul

The detached person is in a position to arrive at a fundamental unity, namely at this place in the soul where the Father bears his Son from eternity in a birth in which human beings in principle take part. But even this unity will necessarily have to seem adjourned. Nevertheless, here there is truly talk of the one life that God is.

'As truly as the Father naturally bears his Son in his single nature, so truly he bears him in the depths of the Spirit, and this is the inner world. Here God's ground is my ground and my ground is God's ground. Here I live from what is most myself, just as God lives from what is most himself. Whoever could look into this ground just for a moment, for this man his thousand marks of minted red gold are no more than a false penny . . . For really, if you think that through profound immersion, pious moods, sweet rapture and exceptional grace you can get more of God than by the fire or in the stable, then you are simply taking God, wrapping his head in a cloak and shoving him under a bench.[2] For anyone who seeks God in a particular "way" may take the way but miss the God who is hidden in this way. But one who seeks God without "ways" grasps God as he is in himself. Such a person lives with the Son and he is life itself' (Q 180, M 50).

This internal unity is not a static event but a happening. It is a becoming, both of God and of human beings. Eckhart has a clear picture of this.

'Many simple people think that they must think of God standing there and themselves standing here. It is not like that. God and I, we are one . . . The working and the becoming is one. If the carpenter does not work, the house does not come into being. When the axe rests, so too does this becoming. God and I, we are one in such a work: he works and I become' (Q 186f., M 56).

God's becoming and human becoming are two sides of one event; as Creator, God gives, and as creatures human beings receive: 'For the creature, being is being-received, for God it is being-given' (LW II, 77). This giving and receiving is a constant event. Both human beings and all creation consist of an incessant becoming, a constant stream from God. Human beings 'receive such a being and this being is like an unbroken stream, in becoming' (LW II, 627).

Outside this ongoing stream of giving and receiving, human beings are nothing. But with this event they are fundamentally one with God, one in becoming. Sometimes Eckhart reinforces the image of the carpenter with that of the artist. The carpenter builds the house from material which is not himself, but the artist reaches as it were into himself, 'into his own life and thought' (LW III, 8), to make his work of art. It is part of himself. However, Eckhart usually uses trinitarian language to describe this oneness in becoming, the language of giving birth and being born. Here is just one example:

'And the Father gives birth to his Son in the soul in the same way as he gives birth to him in eternity and not otherwise. He must do this whether he likes it or whether he suffers. The Father gives birth to his Son without ceasing; and I can say even more: he gives birth to me as his Son and as the same Son. Yet more: he gives birth to me not only as his Son; he gives birth to me as himself and to himself as me, and to me as his being and his nature. In the deepest source I well up in the Holy Spirit; there is one life, one being and one work. All that God does is one; therefore he gives birth to me as his Son, without any distinction' (Q 185, M 55).

The unity of God which is found here is no small one; as Father-Son-Spirit God is the giver of human and worldly reality. With this source, human beings as recipients of the gift aare woven into one event. Both God and human beings become themselves in this surpassing event. But this Christian trinitarian face of God, as creator giver, is not yet definitive. It is adjourned in a new movement of growth. God's unity is postponed again.

IV The breakthrough in the Godhead and the citadel of the soul

As long as God is seen as giver and human beings as recipients, religious growth is still not at an end. For the master-servant relationship which arises from this cannot be the last word.

'When the Son is born, he takes from the Father . . . Recently I pondered whether I should take or want anything from God. I will reflect on this very carefully in myself, for if I should take anything from God, then I would be under God as a servant and in this giving he would be master. But it may not be like that with us in eternal life' (M 55f., Q 186).

1. Letting go of 'God'

So there is something that goes beyond the dynamic God-man relationship in which God is giver and human beings are recipients. It is necessary to let go of God the giver or God the creator precisely for the sake of God. On the human side that conjures up the image of the 'nobility', the 'citadel' or simply the 'something in the soul'. Eckhart sometimes speaks to God of the Godhead. It is clear from the retractions and denials that he is using limit-concepts.

'Therefore I asked God to rid me of God, for my essential being is above God, in so far as we see God as the beginning of creatures' (Q 308, M 98). 'The highest and most extreme of which a man can let go is for him to let go of God for God's sake. St Paul let go of God for God's sake. He let go of all that he could take from God, and he let go of all that God could give him and all that he could receive from God. When he let go of all this, he let go of God for God's sake, and there God remained for him God as God is in himself, thus not in the way in which he is received or gained but in the being that God is in himself. He never gave God anything or received anything from God; it is simply and purely a matter of being one. Here the human being is truly human, and no suffering touches this human being, any more than it touches the divine being. As I have already said often, there is something in the soul that is so related to God that it is one and not unified. It is one, it does not have anything in common with anything, nor does it have anything in common with any thing that is created. All that is created is nothing. Now this something is far from and alien to the createdness of creatures. Were the whole person of this nature, then it would be totally uncreated and uncreatable. Should what is material and breakable be taken up into such a unity, then this would be none other than the unity itself' (Q 214f., M 61f.).

2. Original unity

That 'something in the soul', uncreated and uncreatable, seems to be an element of an original unity with God which human beings carry around in themselves in their creaturely careers. It transcends God as creator. To come into this 'something' or 'citadel', God must leave behind his trinitarian being as creator-giver.

'So totally one and simple is this citadel, and so exalted above all ways and all forces is this unique one, that there can never be a power or a way of looking inwards, not even for God himself. In full truth and thus truly

God lives; God himself will never for a moment look into it, nor has he ever looked into it in so far as he exists in the way and after the property of his persons . . . Rather, just as he is simply one, without any ways or properties, in this sense he is neither Father nor Son nor Holy Spirit and yet he is a something that is not this. Look, just as he is one and simple, he so comes into this one that I call a citadel in the soul. And he does not enter it otherwise in any way. But only in this way does he enter and so he is within' (Q 164, M 41f.).

So there is a unity which lies behind the trinitarian God-creator-giver. Eckhart has this ultimate unity in view when he constantly postpones all kinds of religious homes and also unity-as-event which is really received – both with corresponding images of God. As creator God becomes God in the same way as the carpenter becomes himself in working on the house. 'God' is the name in relation to creatures, but that is not final unity.

'For before creatures were, God was not yet "God": he was rather what he was. When the creatures came into being and thus received their created being, God was not God in himself, but he was God in the creatures. Now we say that God, in so far as he is God, is not the supreme goal of creation' (Q 305, M 96).

3. From God to Godhead

To indicate the issue Eckhart sometimes talks of Godhead. Sometimes he hints at the ultimate unity in metaphors which escape any attempt to grasp them: ground, source, abyss, abysmal darkness. The difference between God and Godhead is not a real difference but a difference of knowing. God and Godhead are not different entities, but different human perspectives. In the recurrent movement from the Spirit, 'God' is by-passed: that is the breakthrough into the Godhead. In speculative language an attempt is made to arrive at the most intimate place in the relationship with God, beyond the place where the relationship is described and interpreted in by the trinitarian receiving and giving.

'Once again I want to say what I have not yet said: God and Godhead are as far from one another as heaven and earth. I say even more: the inner and outer person are as far from one another as heaven and earth. But in God that is many thousand miles more: God "becomes" and "un-becomes" . . . God becomes "God"; where all creatures express God, there God becomes. When I still stood in the ground, in the stream and source of the Godhead, no one asked me where I wanted to go or what I was doing. There was no one who could have asked me these questions. But when I emerged, all the creatures said "God!". If one asked me, "Brother Eckhart, when did you go out of the house", then I was in it. All creatures talk of God in this way. And why do they not speak of the Godhead? All that is in the Godhead is one, and one cannot speak of it. God works, the Godhead does not work, nor does it not have anything to do; in it there is no work, and it has never looked outside for a work' (Q 272, M 79f.).

4. The citadel of the soul

The un-becoming of God the creator is the work of the Spirit who brings the human being-Son home with all things in the abysmal darkness. No one has missed the human being when he returns into the Godhead after his detour, in the breakthrough through the creator God. He is there as though he had not been away; he has brought something of the original home in his coming out. Here lies the indestructible core of the human being which defies all corruptibility, the original unity which has broken through all master-servant relationships with God,[3] although this relationship itself was always a centre of Eckhart's own religious culture: incarnation from God or the birth of God in the soul. This is what Eckhart calls the 'nobility' or the 'citadel' of the soul: 'something' that a human being intrinsically has, an inalienable unity, which is also a property of God.

The ultimate unity, where 'God un-becomes', ultimately escapes any grasp: 'the hidden mystery of his hidden Godhead . . . It is the hidden darkness of the eternal Godhead, and it is unknown and never will be known' (Q 260, M 74). The postponement of this hidden unity makes room for the many faces of God and for the differences in religious life.[4]

Translated by John Bowden

Notes

1. The philosophical concept of causality and theological trinitarian terminology are interwoven. Cf. Sermon 12, LW IV, 14; *In Joh.* 231, LW III 274. Eckhart texts are cited from: 1. *Meister Eckhart, Die deutschen und lateinischen Werke*, ed. for the Deutsche Forschungsgemeinschaft, Stuttgart and Berlin 1936ff. (this edition is abbreviated as DW (Deutsche Werke) or LW (Lateinische Werke), with the volume numbers in Roman and the page numbers in Arabic figures; 2. J. Quint, *Meister Eckehart. Deutsche Predigten und Traktate*, Munich nd (abbreviated as Q); 3. The

Dutch edition, F. Maas, *Van God houden als van niemand. Preken van Eckhart*, Haarlem ²1983 (abbreviated as M).

2. The imagery of God wrapped in a cloak and put under a bench is probably taken from choral prayer; when the time is finished the monks put away their cloaks and breviaries. If one were to attach religion to the 'ways' (times of prayer), then one would also as it were be putting away God.

3. Cf. Q 186, M 55f.; Q 270, M 76f.; Q 273, M 80.

4. Cf. A. Haas, 'Meister Eckhart als Gesprächspartner östlicher Religion', *Freiburg Zeitschrift für Philosophie und Theologie* 34, 1987, 132–45; N. Largier, 'Meister Eckhart und der Osten. Zur Forschungsgeschichte. Bibliographie', ibid., 124–30; J. Zapf, 'Meister Eckhart und die mystische Tradition des Ostens', *Zeitwende* 51, 1980, 2, 102–15; *Meister Eckhart heute*, ed. W. Böhme, Karlsruhe 1980, 57–70; R. Otto, *Mystique d'Orient et mystique d'Occident, Shankara et Maître Eckhart, Bibliothèque scientifique*, Paris 1951; B. Barzel, *Mystique de l'Ineffable dans l'hindouisme et le Christianisme. Shankara et Eckhart*, Paris 1982; R. Schürmann, 'The Loss of the Origin in Soto Zen and Meister Eckhart', *The Thomist* 42, 1978, 281–312; S. Ueda, *Die Gottesgeburt in der Seele und der Durchbruch zur Gottheit. Die mystische Anthropologie Meister Eckharts und ihre Konfrontation mit der Mystik des Zen Buddhismus*, Gütersloh 1965; id., 'Zen Buddhism and Meister Eckhart', in *Zen Buddhism Today. Annual Report of the Kyoto Zen Symposium* 2, 1984, 91–107.

The Relationship with God and Social Conduct

Peter Eicher

'Develop your legitimate strangeness' (René Char)

Just as in mechanical clocks the invisible balance keeps a visible movement going on the face indicating time which is made a norm by society, so the longing for the infinite again and again provokes a form of unresting social conduct. When the balance broke in old clocks, the hands stood still. The digitalized clocks has abolished the balance and made its precise pulses the numbered measure of social conduct. Modern society has privatized the relationship with God and banished its impulses to the unconscious. But in so doing it has discovered that the psyche does not fit into its social norms and in its own growth relates to an ideal self which cannot be realized in society. That has given rise to the paradox that psychoanalysis and depth psychology have demonstrated the universal psychological significance of the symbolism of God at the very moment when sociology regards the privatization of religion as complete. The functions of religion which can still be detected by sociologists evidently do not coincide with its psychological significance, which in modern society has been repressed in the unconscious. So a theology illuminated by psychoanalysis and depth psychology must itself investigate the social significance of that unconscious spiritual dynamic in which the archaic symbols of the relationship with God take on constantly new life.

I. 'Catholicity'

If a society no longer bases its meaning and its norms on symbols for the relationship with God which have a public effect, then priests and theologians, i.e. the bearers of religious power, must react to this privatization of their religion by a rationalization of the religious symbols. In so doing they destroy the unconsciously effective content of the symbolism more persistently than the critics of their religious power ever sought to do. What that means for the Catholic religion is evident to anyone; it can be demonstrated most clearly by means of the term 'Catholic' itself.

'What has been believed everywhere, always and by all – that is catholic in the true and authentic sense.' With this principle of consensus, in the fifth century Vincent of Lérins[1] formulated the decisive argument which justifies the social validity of church symbols to critics outside and within. At least in principle, he thus recognized that the true religion had to base its claim to be the sole vehicle of salvation on collective faith and not the formal authority of the decision-makers. The early church understood itself as the ideal representative of the *salus publicus*, of social well-being, compared with which formal power – as in Augustine – appeared as mere force, indeed as diabolical.

Accordingly, the theology of the first millennium was also marked by a soteriological purging of symbols which related to experience in dealing with myths, rites and processes of healing. In modern terms, it was engaged in a critical discussion of the therapeutic function of archetypal symbolism. The collective experience which all individuals could have introspectively in themselves was the foundation for the revelatory character of their own religion. What was experienced by all as effectively salvific was to be Catholic.

As has been recognized, in modern times Vincent of Lérins' principles came to be read in reverse: what the hierarchical authority declares to be Catholic has to be believed everywhere and at all times by all. The old relationship between revelation and collective experience has been literally stood on its head in the battle of the old hierarchy against the new natural sciences, against reformation, political absolutism and social enlightment. The head of the church visible to all the world, which is what pope and bishops now claimed to be in Christ's place, took over the whole power of defining what was 'Catholic'. And precisely in this way the Catholic confession marked itself off from the collective experience of the salvific and opposed the unconscious dynamic of universal religious symbolism. This bureaucratization of salvation not only led to Catholicity being experienced as an increasingly relative section of human life, but increasingly also meant that the norms ordained by the pope for 'authentic' democracy,[2] for 'normal' sexual behaviour, for the 'true' significance of woman and the 'only valid' interpretation of the Bible were also felt by individuals to be increasingly disastrous. The unfulfilled longing for a God of all human beings which could be demonstrated from the symbols of a creative ground of all experience, redeeming and loving, was not compensated for by the authoritarian norms of the Roman Catholic collective.

Two dimensions above all are suppressed in this authoritarian ideology in the link between the relationship with God and social conduct. First, the magisterial authority fails to recognize the symbolic character of any experience of God as this has been plausibly demonstrated by psycho-analysis, depth psychology and the study of religion. And secondly, it violates the social rule which is the presupposition for its own argument on the basis of religious freedom: it abuses the autonomy of social action by failing in its authoritarian regulations to observe the basic obligation of any free, i.e. any good action. Because both dogmatically and moralistically it fails to do justice to the collective content of its own experience of God, it socially reinforces the authoritarian character of family, society and state and thus encourages their potential for aggression. As is well known, no social conflicts are waged so cruelly as those waged with divine authority.

II. Symbolic time

Now in fact an analysis of the unconscious discloses a basic set of experiences which are had 'everywhere and always by all'. The problem is that both depth psychology and sociology concede that these collective experiences present themselves with a notable lack of sharpness and strongly resist translation into rational consciousness. Granted, only part of the unconscious dynamic also develops a religious symbolism, but all religious behaviour is grounded in the transference of unconscious identifications into universal ideals and conflicts. For this reason alone, the functional outside approach to religions which has been characteristic of sociology from the start can never coincide with the self-understanding of believers. To the degree that all religious experiences are rooted in the individual and collective dynamic of the psyche, they evade any socio-logical understanding. Functional sociology notes the symptoms of the religious dynamic of the unconscious without developing their significance, in the same way as medical actuaries deal with illnesses. It can only perceive the conscious transferences and not their unconscious ground.[3]

The dynamic of the unconscious, which is essentially situated in the limbic system of the medulla, has developed over two million years of evolution. Not only does it determine around six-sevenths of all human experience; it also shapes the affects far more strongly than conscious reflection.[4] From the perspective of depth psychology, what essentially emerges in the experiences of dreaming and in the complex feelings of everyday life, in suffering from neurotic symptoms and in the material of myths and fairy-tales, in art, literature and the dream factory of films, derives from this universal dynamic which makes symbolic experience possible. The universal religious symbols (flesh, water and light, eye, hand and word, heaven and hell, breath and spirit, father, son and mother) reflect the constancy of universal transference from the unconscious dynamic into a reality which can be depicted, even if every culture speaks its own dialect of this universal language. In the religions, the central symbols of the unconscious are given a social interpretation, experienced collectively, and made social norms.

In this view the religions appear as the social memory of the universal symbolic experience which stems from the collective dynamic of the unconscious. They are the inculturations of the individual and collective dynamic of the universal images of the unconscious as these have taken shape in history. Any conscious interpretation of this symbolic experience by dogma, morality and science tempers the glowing masses of lava from this unconscious volcano of religious passions with the coolness of its reason: the interpretation of the unconscious dynamic translates the symbol into the language of the prevailing culture and adapts its 'irrational' part to the rules of social behaviour. The flesh, the eye or the spirit which 'are' God for an Australian tribal culture or for Christian faith do not mean what dogma or science can say about them. In a manner which is ultimately inexpressible they represent in a healthy or a threatening way the 'embodiment', the 'manifestation' or the 'election' which unconsciously determine existence as a whole. The symbols say what they mean without really being capable of translation. And as they derive from the unconscious, they are also understood unconsciously.

The dilemma of any scientific explanation of relationships with God thus remains: what is transferred affectively in religious experience to human beings of all times and places and to the cosmos and its divine origin as a whole remains largely unconscious and can be depicted only in symbols – what is brought to consciousness from this is reflected through the language, culture and social norms of the particular interpreters. The universal symbols of the relationship with God triumph over their social meaning. And it is precisely this which constitutes their social significance.

There are three points which make this understanding of the unconscious by depth psychology at least plausible for an analysis of the link between the relationship with God and social conduct.

1. The double existence: social conduct and dreams

Anyone can see by experiment how the link between religious experience and social conduct does not take place simultaneously. It is enough to note some of the structural characteristics of one's own dreams. In dreams, socialized individuals turn into other-worldly doubles of themselves. In play they overcome the limits of time and space. Not only can they leave their own bodies like shamans or watch themselves dying; they can also meet the dead and experience the future in anticipation. In its dreams the psyche first of all transcends and abolishes the linear time which is constitutive of all social action. In the eternal return of the same, the psyche exchanges the present for the past or future and allows the sleeping person to exist in dream-time.[5] The limits of space also become transparent: the place which dreamers can enter can be anywhere or nowhere. The objects and remnants of social experience seem to take on animistic movement in dreams. And finally, in dreams actions are played out as though the morality, laws and social rules of everyday life did not exist. The irreversibility of the social actions which grow out of social ties and obligations loses its compelling validity every night.

2. The vagabond psyche

Whereas the self when awake essentially owes its consistency and power of organization to the contemporaneity with the rules of social behaviour which it has laboriously learned, the dreaming soul is a vagabond, without having had to learn to be, through heaven and hell, through seas and skies, through paradises and abysses, as though its kingdom were not of this world. The human self exists in the contrary doubling of dream-time and real time. As in Indian logic, it is at the same time both what it is and what it is not. For as the dream sequences are also continued or brought to consciousness in the waking state, human beings always have a double existence: in the unconscious of the psyche of their self which breaks through the simultaneous social experiences, and as a social 'I' which is obligated to the prevailing order of the day. In dream-time this hardness of everyday experience is radically relativized.

Phenomenologists of religion and depth psychologists have now consolidated the hypothesis of this psychological theory of relativity according to which the symbolic objectivations in rites and myths, in religious dance and the notions of faith, correspond to the symbols of dream-time. They emerge universally because in dreaming, fundamental affective experiences of the socialization of early childhood recur in the individual unconscious in the same way as basic phylogenetic experiences emerge from the collective dynamic of the unconscious. There are close analogies between the dynamic of dream symbols and the dynamic sequences of images in myths, rites and notions of faith, which psychologists can understand.

It is no coincidence that the symbol of paradise, which is distributed universally, correlates with the symbiotic feeling of primary intimacy in the womb. The sequences of images of a flood from which an ark provides rescue, which recur in all cultures, correspond to the dream symbols of regression and deliverance. A symbolic pair like Cain and Abel appears not only in all mythologies but also in the unconscious dream images of sibling conflict. The sacrifice of the son which is commanded and prevented by the deity corresponds to the aggressive images in the father-son conflict. The exodus from the house of slavery picks up the fundamental dynamic which in the service of genetic development drives each new generation to forsake the primary intimacy and to look for its own way of dealing with the mountain of the law. The symbolism of the divine father and a divine mother image is no more absent from religions than from the regressive or prospective dreams of individuals. And even the basic symbolism of Christianity, the new creation of the earth from the nothingness of chaos, the incarnation of the divine ideal, the death and resurrection of the cult hero, the sending of the spirit from heaven and the return of the saviour correspond to a culturally universal symbolism which for its part finds a parallel at all times in the unconscious dynamic of dreams of descent into death and rebirth to life.

3. The significance of the relationship with God

The symbols of dream-time refuse to comply with the real time of social experience and make men and women beings who exist in different times. In religions this lack of simultaneity is experienced collectively and given a social interpretation in the framework of their historical culture. The way from the beyond of this dream-time into this world of social time is similarly presented in a symbolic way (in the myth, narrative and symbolism of faith) and is brought to consciousness in the opposite direction (in rites, sacraments and therapeutic spiritual direction). Thus the expression 'symbol' means essentially the coming together of that which is not simultaneous. At their most intense, the manifest symbols of the relationship with God (sacrifice, the eating of flesh and drinking of blood, dancing, festivals and pilgrimage, incubation, trances and ecstasy, washing and the pains of initiation, totem and tabu, the prohibition of images and sacred texts, sacraments and acts of confession) represent the simultaneity of what is radically not simultaneous.

This is no more decisive for the being of God *per se* than it is for the influence which the symbolic experience has on social conduct (and vice versa). But the fundamental significance of the relationship with God does become clear: the relationship with God rooted in the unconscious embraces social conduct (as Durkheim pointed out) and breaks open everyday time from within (as Max Weber pointed out). It can be presented symbolically only because its conscious dogmatic or moral fixation has already lost its own 'return of the same' to the linear time of a society which orientates itself on the constancy of work and its products.

What in the everyday life of society[6] is brief and has to be worked out is given fully and quite gratuitously in dream-time. In the light of the unconscious, what in social adaptation is experienced as banal routine or has to be laboriously attained by virtue can appear as the drama of a murderous conflict – just as, conversely, the unconscious encounter with the star of redemption, the blue flower, the tree of life or a sage can produce physical redemption. But the dynamic of symbols works very strongly against socially experienced contingency: what is real appears in dreams as possible, and what in reality is only possible is already experienced in dream-time as real. The dynamic of the unconscious has a revolutionary effect as a source of utopia: its imaginative power bursts through any social and biological time. In the 'little death' of sleep, social reality dies, and a fundamentally new world arises in which, in an unconscious vision, even death itself can be experienced. Without dream-time there would be no experience of God, even if this is more than a dream.

III. The healing of socially caused suffering

The healing power of a religion essentially depends on its capacity to come into contact with the unconscious and work through the projections which emerge from the unconscious.[7] Here, it is not enough for the divided ideals and aggressions of the unconscious to be represented symbolically, as for example in the ideas of the ascension and the descent into hell, the battle between God and the devil. Religious symbolism mitigates suffering and furthers enjoyment of life only if it is confronted within the framework of organized religion with the harshness of everyday experience, social conditions, and the contingency of existence.

1. The praxis of the religions

Whereas in shamanistic cultures this healthy confrontation consists in the diagnosis of dreams and the vicarious dream journey of the shaman, for Buddhist illumination everything depends on a state of suspension in relation to both the projected powers and authorities and reality as a whole. The wheel of enlightenment frees from suffering step by step by detaching existence from inner dependence on the power of nature and social oppression; the way to what is by being nothing (Nirvana) completely dissolves the projective idealization and demonization of nature and society as quasi-divine effective powers. For Buddhism, there is no redemption from the cycle of reality, which is occupied by desires, without also completely working through the projective character of the ultimate notion of all the dynamics of the soul, the notion of heaven and hell, of God and the devil's dragon, indeed of eternal rebirth.

Nor is it too much to characterize Islam as the religion which applies the revealed order of law revealed to Muhammad in the supreme waking dream as a norm for social conduct, and allows the life of the believer at the same time to be experienced as 'the living of a dream'.[8] Both faith and doing right are grounded in the conviction that only those who know themselves can have a right relationship to the only true God. However, in Islam, self-knowledge is gained through a much stronger empathy with dream-time than is the case in orthodox Judaism and in that form of Christianity which has a deep dogmatic stamp. That orthodoxy has not yet fully worked through this subjectification for legal guidance is shown by the politically precarious deficit in the relationship between Islam and more open societies.

Orthodox Judaism and mainstream Christianity have preserved their relationship to the God who is at the same time both manifest and hidden right down to the twentieth century without relating their symbol of the one God who reveals himself through prophets or 'the Son' to the unconscious dynamic of the psyche. This led rabbinic Judaism to attempt as far as possible to shape the social life of its people amidst hostile nations by strict reference to the Torah (halakhah) and its own history (haggadah). Right down to the reform Judaism of the Enlightenment, keeping a social distance from the 'host' nations necessarily remained the sign of a true relationship with God. As indicated at the beginning of this article, by contrast Christianity has rationalized its relationship to society to a considerable degree, so that at the end of the twentieth century it finds itself restricted to a presence in society as a higher moral authority, as the vehicle of dogmatic truths and as a hierarchical bearer of rites.

2. The faith of the fathers: Freud and Jung

It is hardly a coincidence that the impetus towards a renewed exploration of the unconscious dynamic of the relationship to God came from Jewish psychiatrists and then the son of a Protestant pastor. No one has recognized the laws of this return of the suppressed more accurately than the men and women who were themselves the heirs of highly rationalized Judaism or Christianity. The scheme for psychoanalysis produced by Sigmund Freud and the working out of depth psychology by Carl Gustav Jung can both be read as the psychological elucidation of the 'faith of the fathers'.[9] At the centre of this elucidation stands the therapeutic relationship of the unconscious to social behaviour. The assessment of the social function of religious symbolism is governed here essentially by dream theory.

Sigmund Freud worked out his discovery of the unconscious above all through the interpretation of dreams, on which he worked all his life. According to this, the symbolic scenes in dreams fulfil for individuals the desires which are denied them by nature and culture, but this fulfilment remains illusory. The affective strength of this illusion derives from the symbiotic sense of narcissism in early infancy, which continues in dreams. With all the clarity that could be desired, Freud compared the affective strengths of religious symbolism with what happens in dreams and learned to understand both dreams and religion genetically from the same drives. But it was the permissiveness and aggressiveness of dream journeys every night which for Freud showed once and for all that 'every individual is virtually an enemy of civilization, though civilization is supposed to be an object of universal human interest . . . This civilization has to be defended against the individual'.[10] Certainly because of their ideal formations the religions represent a 'high point' of culture. However, they remain hostile to a society shaped by science because like dreams they obey the wish-principle, and not the social awareness of reality which has been attained in the meantime.

Freud saw as particularly hostile a retention of religious idealizations which become the motive force of aggression against all who threaten the ideal.[11] So he could regard the 'oceanic feeling' of the eternal and unlimited offered to him by Romain Rolland[12] as just as harmful as what was in his view the unnatural requirement to love neighbour and love enemy: 'If I love someone, he must deserve it in some way . . . But if I am to love him (with this universal love) merely because he, too, is an inhabitant of this earth, like an insect, an earthworm or a grass snake, then I fear that only a small modicum of my love will fall to his share . . . Not merely is this stranger in general unworthy of my love; I must honestly confess that he has more claim to my hostility and even my hatred; . . if he can satisfy any desire by it, he thinks nothing of jeering at me, insulting me, slandering me and showing his superior power . . ."[13] It was the harshness of experience which drove Freud as a Jew to require the 'wild beast' to reject idealized wishes and energetically to renounce desires. Only in commitment to a scientific culture can the disenchanted person work towards resignation.

Romain Rolland, who because of the First World War argued as a pacifist for a gospel of universl love for all earthly beings (including grass snakes and earthworms), and of whom Freud was therefore a lifelong admirer, protested to his admirer that as a psychoanalyst Freud only entered the unlimited world of the unconscious as a stranger and practised an almost religious renunciation of religion.[14] In so doing he gave a very precise formulation of the starting point for Carl Gustav Jung's complex analysis of the dream world and thus of religion.

Jung did not understand dreams in terms of the hypothesis of a biologically active drive; on the contrary, he attempted to understand the dynamic of the soul from the dream images. At the same time he wanted not to explain religion through a psychoanalytical foreknowledge but to approach the understanding of the psyche first of all through the symbolism of religion. One of his decisive insights into the link between the relationship with God and social behaviour was that the religious images of the soul cannot be reduced to individual development, but unfold a collective dynamic which is peculiar to human beings generally. The anticipatory character of these collective wishes makes it possible to understand religions in depth, which not only allows one to understand them better – from their unconscious roots – and to come nearer to them in human terms, but also shows that they are defenders of individual and human needs against the economic, political and military demands of societies. The infinite idealization which from a psychological perspective makes up the relationship with God can distance individuals in a rational way from the pressure of social compulsions. As Jung's wanderings in the German myths of the Nazis shows,[15] trust in the power of symbols can also blind people politically. However, Jung himself never ceased to emphasize that only by constantly working through even religious symbols rationally can one eliminate their destructive effect. But what seemed to him even more destructive was a social consciousness which regarded the permanent working-through of symbols as superfluous.

3. Appropriation of religion

But what happens once the psychological genesis of the relationship with God has been recognized and the projection of one's own symbiotic wishes on a God outside one's own consciousness has been worked through? Then, Erich Fromm thinks, there is a truly humane appropriation of religion. Religious feeling which has become humane dispenses with any authoritarian and dogmatic claim to reality and contents itself with the active experience of the divine in itself.[16] Eugen Drewermann's work points in this direction, because he understands the symbols of Christianity neither as a reflection of (past) social conditions nor as assertions about fact, but 'as the objective structure of the subjective'.[17] Then and only then can the subjective recognition of one's own relationship with God still the despair of finite existence and reinforce the social autonomy of believers, if they dare to trust in the objective power of symbols. Neither the public rite of a religion nor its dogmatic self-assertion and special ethical demands are enough for this, because all this leads religion to be experienced merely as a rather more rigorous or more premodern part of society itself. For this it is enough simply to encounter a fellow human being who in an encounter free from anxiety helps one to understand oneself rightly from the unconscious dynamic of the self. To this degree, love of God and love of neighbour are constituent parts of each other. Their connection first makes possible the 'unsatisfied enlightenment' of the autonomous subject so that it really recognizes the self in society and in the relationship with the absolute. The art of a religion which does not allow the relationship to God to be submerged in social conduct is that it ventures this move into the uncontemporaneity of the contemporaneous. It is the art of faith which all the time has to work out its ideal through reality.

However, a relationship with God which shut up the subject in its psychological dream-time would remain the worst consolation for the soul. The criteria for true and false religion first emerge in the dispute over the power with which the ensouled subject can in fact change the repressive structures of society. For just as social conditions damage the psyche, so a privatized religion of the soul damages society. The vicious circle can only be broken by active perception of the symbols which encourage believers of all religions together to approach in radical political terms the central questions of war, ecology and above all the increasing violence of economic exploitation.

IV. The rite: symbol or representation of power?

An everyday example can demonstrate where the strongest challenge to a critical symbolism lies. In a German diocese a church minister[18] was suspended immediately because he wrote the memorable sentence: 'The dialogical disclosure of the message of the gospel, the affirmation of the participation of all, both men and women, in worship without respect of race, confession or religion, makes possible a trusting encounter of people of the most varied kinds in table-fellowship.'[19]

Table-fellowship is the basic symbolism of a hospitality which allows strangers in a place, too, to renew their own lives. The gospel – in line with criticism of the temple – has replaced the bloody sacrificial altar with the ordinary table. It stands as a commemoration of the table-fellowship of Jesus with the socially marginalized, as a symbol of the place of reconciliation and as an eschatological sign of the communion of all peoples in all churches. The dogma and canon law of the Roman Catholic hierarchy have made this central symbol of union a place of separation from strangers. What that means for society is obvious to all.

Translated by John Bowden

Notes

1. Vincent of Lérins, *Commonitorium*, 2.3.

2. Cf. the encyclical *Veritatis splendor* of 6 August 1993, nos. 96–100; for his norms John Paul II also referred to Vincent of Lérins, cf. no. 53 of the encyclical.

3. This is impressively shown by the discussion in P. Koslowski, *Die religiöse Dimension der Gesellschaft. Religion and ihre Theorien*, Tübingen 1985.

4. Cf. K. Wezler, 'Menschliches Leben in der Sicht der Physiologie', in H. G. Gadamer and P. Vogler (eds.), *Neue Anthropologie*, Vol. 2, *Biologische Anthropologie II*, Stuttgart 1972, 292–386.

5. In his basic ethnological study, H. P. Duerr, *Traumzeit*, Frankfurt am Main 1978, [2]1985, has substantiated the thesis that every culture creates for itself in a shamanistic way institutions which allow it access to an outside radically different from itself, to a dream-time. J. Assmann, 'Der zweidimensionale Mensch: das Fest als Medium des kollektiven Gedächtnis', in id. (ed.), *Das Fest und das Heilige*, Gütersloh 1991, 13–31: 19, proposed that the term 'dream-time' should be used generally for the other as opposed to the everyday, thus for example for festival time. The ethnological restriction to the shamanistic institution remains too narrow by comparison with the basic experience, and the historical perspective is too broad. History and theology cannot ignore the psychoanalytical analysis of dreams if they want to understand shamanistic, cultural or liturgical dream-time adequately. However, for its part, depth psychology cannot make prior decisions about the ethnological, historical or theological

interpretation of symbols, because it remains limited to the time of the unconscious and thus the pre-social.

6. For what follows see the ethnological analyses in F. Kramer and C Sigrist (eds.), *Gesellschaften ohne Staat*, 2, *Genealogie und Solidarität*, Frankfurt am Main 1978; Assmann, *Das Fest und das Heilige* (n. 5).

7. For what follows see the studies in R. Caillois and G. E. Grunebaum, *Le rêve et les sociétés humaines*, Paris 1967; P. Harvey, *An Introduction to Buddhism. Teachings, History and Practices*, Cambridge 1990.

8. F. Rahman, 'Le rêve, l'imagination et 'Alam Al-Mithal', in Caillos and Grunebaum, *Le rêve et les sociétés humaines* (n. 7), 407–25: 407.

9. Cf. P. Gay, *A Godless Jew: Freud, Atheism and the Making of Psychoanalysis*, New Haven and London 1987; Y. H. Yerushalmi, *Freud's Moses. Judaism Terminable and Interminable*, New Haven and London 1991; C. G. Jung, *Memories, Dreams, Reflections*, ed. A. Jaffé, London and New York 1967: R. Höfer, *Die Hiobsbotschaft C. G. Jungs. Folgen sexuellen Missbrauchs*, Lüneburg 1993; for a comparable transformation in Jacques Lacan, cf. E. Roudinesco, *Jacques Lacan. Esquisse d'une vie, histoire d'un système de pensée*, Paris 1993.

10. S. Freud, 'The Future of an Illusion in Civilization, Society and Religion', Penguin Freud Library, Vol. 12, Harmondsworth 1985, 179–242: 184.

11. For a psychoanalytical deepening of this important insight in the relationship between religion and society also cf. T. Bauriedl, *Wege aus der Gewalt. Analyse von Beziehungen*, Freiburg im Breisgau ²1992.

12. S. Freud, 'Civilization and its Discontents', ibid., 243–340: 261; cf. M. Hulin, *La mystique sauvage*, Paris 1993, 19–34.

13. Ibid., 299f.

14. Cf. Hulin, *La mystique sauvage* (n. 12), 31f.

15. Cf. T. Evers, *Mythos und Emanzipation, Eine kritische Annäherung an C. G. Jung*, Hamburg 1987.

16. For the sociological discussion cf. B. Bierhoff, *Erich Fromm. Analytische Sozialpsychologie und visionäre Gesellschaftskritik*, Darmstadt 1993.

17. E. Drewermann, *Glauben in Freiheit oder Tiefenpsychologie und Dogmatik*, I, *Dogma, Angst und Symbolismus*, Solothurn and Düsseldorf 1993, 400.

18. Here I want to pay my respects to Peter Neuhaus, the college chaplain in Siegen, who despite measures taken by the Archbishop of Paderborn, Johannes Joachim Degenhardt, feels a duty to show simultaneous love of both God and neighbour.

19. *Publik-Forum* 23, 1994, no. 11, 28f.

The Feminine Face of God

Helen Schüngel-Straumann

The biblical tradition, by which all talk of God must allow itself to be measured, speaks of God in predominantly male language. This is a problem not only of the language but above all of the structures of the society of the time, in both the Old Testament and the New Testament periods. Here Christian notions are shaped more by the New Testament than by the Hebrew Bible in an androcentric way of talking of God, because in the New Testament God as the Father of Jesus Christ appears in clearly male terminology. But if we look more closely at the way in which Jesus depicts his 'Father' and the way in which he talks to him, it is evident that this is not as androcentric, as reduced to the male measure, as it might seem at first sight. Thus for example it is significant that the mother is missing in, say, the parable of the prodigal son. In this 'family' the kind father has wholly taken over the role of the mother; he has the strength even to overcome the anger which is usually assigned to the paternal role.

I. God as Father in the Old Testament

Only if we look from the New Testament back into the Old is the image of the father also introduced there at some points – almost imperceptibly. The result of this is that other images and symbols for God are often no longer really perceived, because this one-sided perspective distorts realities. Here I shall be discussing some of the very numerous references in the Old Testament which either break up or relativize a picture of God with a male stamp, above all the feminine notion of the *ruaḥ* (wind, breath, spiritual force, creative force). But first of all we must look at the image of the father or its alternatives in the Old Testament. It is striking that the Old Testament is extremely sparing with the concept of father. When we remember that the Old Testament writings came into being over a period

of around a thousand years, it is amazing that God is spoken of as 'father' at
most in a dozen passages. Here we should note that no sexualization of God is
intended with this designation; it emphasizes the aspects of responsibility
and care. For a patriarchal society it is amazing that there is no stronger
emphasis here on paternal authority. The aspect of care in particular is also
covered in maternal images and concepts, especially as we find them in
Deutero- and Trito-Isaiah, and also in Hosea (Isa. 49.15; 66.13; Hos. 11).

II. God as mother in Hosea 11[1]

The pre-understanding that in this prophet God is portrayed as father can
be found in all the commentaries, but it does not do justice to the text. It
already goes back to the evangelist Matthew, who interprets the first
statement 'Out of Egypt I called my son' (Hos. 11.1) typologically with
reference to Jesus in the story of the flight of the holy family to Egypt
(Matt. 2.14). This clearly indicates that Jesus is thought of as the son, and
God as the father. But Hosea has a quite different statement: in ch. 11 we
have the 'wisdom of his old age', the quintessence of a long and painful
prophetic life which was shaped by disappointments and failure. It is clear
to Hosea that Israel has deserved this downfall and that the imminent end
is the retribution it gets for its behaviour.

In vv. 1–4 we are told more about how this deity treats Israel, the son:
like a small child, a baby who is looked after, breast-fed and brought up by
his mother. Both v. 3 and v. 4 clearly indicate that the child has constantly
to be given some food. But babies do not eat, but are breast-fed, up to the
age of about three. So here we certainly have no image of a father, but the
image of a mother who is rearing her son – literally. Yahweh treats Israel
like a tender mother, but Israel turns away.

Verses 5–7 depict the consequence of this break, namely the downfall of
Israel through war. They end with the desperate words:

'My people are bent on turning away from me;
they call to Baal,
but he never rears them.'

So what the mother does and can do, namely rear the child, is denied to
Yahweh's adversary, the masculine Baal. He does not do this, nor can he.

It is worth noting in this passionate speech that even in this hopeless
situation Yahweh still addresses Israel as 'my people'; this *my* expresses his
concern, his love, which he does not take back. That ends the first part of
the text, which refers back to the beginning.

In the second part, from v. 8 on, we find a great change. Here God is having an internal struggle, asking passionate questions:

'How can I give you up, Ephraim?
How can I hand you over, Israel?'

In Hosea's time the consequences that Israel has merited here can only be defined as *masculine*. They would be punishment, destruction, and would be spelled out in terms like 'give up', 'hand over', 'ruin', 'inflict fiery wrath' and 'destroy'. However, Yahweh distances himself from precisely this masculine attitude. His heart, which pleads for this child, turns against it, and as a parallel the same thing is said of his womb.[2]

'My heart recoils within me,
my womb is utterly aflame.'

At this point there is a close, almost literal, parallel in I Kings 3.26, in the story of the wise judgment of Solomon, who gives the right child to the right mother. When the king wants to cut the living child in two, the story says of the right mother: 'Her womb burned within her and she said. "Oh my lord, give her the living child and by no means slay it"' (I Kings 3.26). The verb used here describes powerful emotion. It is not possible for the right mother to look on while her child is cut in two. It is not possible for Yahweh to leave this son Israel to be destroyed: this emotional force which is within the very being of God is directed at God's self. This is a kind of revolt, an upheaval within Yahweh, which cannot allow just punishment to be inflicted on Yahweh's own flesh and blood.

We have the reason for this upheaval in v. 9, the climax of this text.

'For I am God (*'el*),
and not man (*'iš*),
the holy One in your midst,
and I do not come to destroy.'

Here God dissociates himself from the masculine conduct which would be just and indeed to be expected, because he is *'el* = God and not *'iš* = man. Here God is not depicting general human behaviour, from which Yahweh dissociates himself, but specifically male behaviour. Because of the ambiguity of the term 'man', this is not always recognized in translations.

Here Hosea depicts a Yahweh who is not a judge, not a righteous, punitive or angry God, but is wholly 'other' ('holy', i.e. removed, of another kind). This deity is concerned to save its relationship more than to present itself, more than to be proud, right, to establish itself, be consistent and show its power. Indeed Yahweh here proves to be immeasurably consistent. This Yahweh is anything but almighty; rather, here we have a deity who has condescended and gone so far as to prefer surrender and being stripped rather than allow Israel to suffer the same fate.

So for this prophet, Yahweh as mother proves to be a valid picture of God, just as in other passages he uses the problematic image of Yahweh as husband. Hosea is very fond of working with pairs of opposites. Here he has divided the male-female polarity in such a way that Yahweh stands over against the male child (boy, son) as mother. He uses a similar opposition in other passages, e.g. Hos. 13.8, where Yahweh uses the comparison of a she-bear robbed of her young. So for this prophet a female-maternal image of God is as valid and legitimate as a male one. But whereas the image of Yahweh as husband and Israel as (unfaithful) wife – Hosea is in fact the prophet who created this picture – went on to have a long and influential history, with in part extremely misogynistic features, the other image of Yahweh as mother was not taken seriously nor accepted.

Here evidently at the end of his long period of activity, where ch. 11 belongs, Hosea has experienced that male images of God are of doubtful viability. In the hopeless situation before the final collapse of the northern kingdom (722/21 BCE), the prophet takes up images which are better suited to express his last and deepest experiences with Yahweh the God of Israel. Only in Yahweh's maternal love does the prophet see a last chance for his people.

Something similar can also be seen around 200 years later, after the collapse of the southern kingdom (587/86 BCE): Deutero- and Trito-Isaiah use similar female-maternal pictures to raise up the desperate people again. They find these better suited to offer help, hope and consolation at a time of catastrophe. Thus the maternal pictures of God are an expression of the experience and maturity of certain prophets, for they, too, are children (mostly male) of their age, who learn and undergo processes of maturing.

It is therefore necessary to emphasize the multiplicity of the images of God. It is not the uniformity but this multiplicity of symbols and designations of God which is suited to describing God appropriately, since God cannot be spoken of other than in images. Thus it is as legitimate to address God as mother as to address God as father, provided that one remains aware that both are images which in their totality are not meant to exclude the other part. The divine shows itself with different faces, and depending on the time and circumstances sometimes the paternal, sometimes the maternal face of God seems more helpful. Here no one-sided re-sexualization of the concept of God is intended, nor simply a reversal of the previous androcentric view.

However, it is legitimate to ask critically whether in talk of the motherliness or fatherliness of God there is not a danger of the mother being so to speak 'incorporated' into the father. Only if one can talk of both the 'motherly father' (as Jürgen Moltmann does) and of the 'fatherly mother' is the danger avoided of the male once again being assumed to be the fundamental characteristic into which the female is 'integrated'. That would once again express a male claim to superiority, only slightly relativized by talk of 'God as mother'.

III. Interpretations of Genesis 1–3[3]

That the male is the criterion and the female only supplementary, or is defined in terms of difference from the male, is usually a result of the old story in Gen. 2 and 3, which is often interpreted in misogynistic terms. The fact that the woman was created from the man and for him (Gen. 2.18ff.) in fact forms the pattern not only for the image of human beings but also for the image of God. Today there is also a wider realization that the stories of the creation of human beings do not seek either to depict historical facts or to define the way in which human beings were created. Rather, the theological writer wants to describe how closely man and woman belong together, a description which culminates in the man's exclamation:

This at last is bone of my bones and flesh of my flesh! (Gen. 2.23).

Although the intention of this story has meanwhile become known, the basic pattern of the priority, indeed the superiority, of the man is retained – often even unconsciously. Even where a naive interpretation of the old narrative is explicitly repudiated, the conclusions which have been drawn from it have been preserved, to the detriment of women and their possibilities for development, and also to the detriment of belief in God, which in this way loses its effective force and is rejected by many women as one-sided, indeed discriminatory.

For the statements in Gen. 1 about the creation of man and woman in the image of God can also be read in such a way as to indicate that God must be contained in both, male and female. If human beings are in principle 'male' and 'female' images of God only in their formation, then this anthropological statement must also have effects on the image of God.

Woman and man are such as reflect the divine; so they must also have a primal image in the divine. So in the light of Gen. 1.26–28 we must also exclude the possibility of regarding the God of the Old Testament as purely male.

However, since in the whole history of theology down to the Enlightenment the text of Gen. 1 was read against the background of the exegesis of the older narratives of Gen. 2 and 3, though the statements about woman being in the image of God were not wholly denied, they were at least abbreviated. The pre-understanding of the superiority and the priority of the man in creation made it difficult to see the careful statement made by so evocatively theological a text as Gen. 1. For the exegetes who became established and formed theological schools were almost exclusively males, who had an interest in maintaining the traditional hierarchies.

This reference to the connection between image of God and image of human beings should have made it clear that the question of the image of God cannot be seen in isolation. The symbols and the language are largely androcentric, so the dominance of the male model must be demolished, in order to free the image of God, too, from its one-sidedness. The neglect of the Old Testament or the view that the Old Testament is to be read only in the light of the New Testament still forms a basic problem for the narrowing of the image of God. Here the fact that the Old Testament contains a wealth of images and experiences of God going beyond the New Testament, not available to the New Testament simply because of the shorter period during which it came into being, is lost sight of. By virtue of its great concreteness and its solid language drawn from human experience and history, the Old Testament offers numerous stimuli and corrections which are particularly necessary today.[4] So not only must the Old Testament be read in the light of the New, but conversely the New Testament should again be read more often against the background of the Old, which as we know was in fact Jesus' Holy Scripture. However, this presupposes that it should be made more widely known, so that it can stimulate and enrich the Christian image of God and open up new perspectives.

IV. Non-personal images of God

Now the symbolism of 'mother' and 'father' remains completely within the sphere of the family. Taken by itself this would again be too one-sided and would fall short, since numerous areas would be omitted. But over and above the impersonal designations of God like 'light', 'source of life', etc., the Old Testament also contains purely feminine images for the divine.

ruaḥ[5]

Here the Hebrew term *ruaḥ* plays an important role. It denotes God's creative lifegiving force which imparts movement, liveliness, to other things; moreover in the early church it was understood to be quite central. At the 'birth' of the church as this is depicted in Peter's preaching at Pentecost (Acts 2), this notion from the Hebrew Bible is used to express the new experiences and cope with them theologically. The maternal image of birth – on this day the young church for the first time becomes public – is not at all coincidental. For at the centre of Peter's sermon are statements about the Spirit derived from the Old Testament. In the first chapters of Acts, Luke reports how this power descends on all, on the men and women who have assembled, and he describes this event as a storm or a rushing wind which brings about a comprehensive understanding: each person hears the others speaking in her or his own language. As in the Old Testament text from the prophet Joel (fourth century BCE) which is quoted, the effects of this *ruaḥ* are described in a threefold way: first, sons and daughters will speak prophetically, i.e. the differences of gender will be done away with in prophesying; secondly, old and young are put on the same footing as far as their visionary-prophetic functions are concerned, i.e. the difference between the generations falls away; and finally the differences in status no longer exist: the relationship between master and servant is no more. All receive the same *ruaḥ*. So the outpouring of the Spirit has a democratizing, liberating effect on all. All men and women are equal under this power of God.

Like Luke, John, too, draws on Old Testament imagery when in the conversation with Nicodemus he makes Jesus say:

> Unless one is born of water and the Spirit,
> he cannot enter the kingdom of God (John 3.5).

Granted, John is writing at the end of the first century, in Greek, like Luke and speaks of *pneuma*, but in both the Semitic origin of the feminine *ruaḥ* idea is clear. The whole background of the biblical notion of spirit is feminine, in total contrast to more modern terms which tend to conceal the original liveliness. Just as in John 3 the power of the Spirit promises new life, so in John 14 it makes it possible for the disciples, male and female, really to understand.

What kind of a force is it which has such a comprehensive effect and is so important that without it the church could not grow nor faith exist? In the Old Testament there was reflection on the need for and effectiveness of the age-old notion of the *ruah*, especially during the period of crisis at the exile. At a time when hopelessness was prevalent and there seemed to be no future, the prophet Ezekiel describes how new life and new hope become possible through the divine *ruah*. In his vision, in which he sees a field of dead bones which are quite dry (Ezek. 37), he speaks of a *ruah* which in very different ways – as wind, as power, as human vitality, and finally also as Yahweh's ownmost spirit – gives new life, new perspectives and also a renewed way of life. In this great vision the prophet makes the concept of *ruah* shine through in many different ways: thus *ruah* is a force which cannot be grasped and cannot be defined. It can be experienced only in its workings, as a force which creates power, liveliness, totality and integrity, which brings about a new joy in life, new verve and courage. This *ruah* is so overpowering that it can bring dead, dried-out bones to life again. This is the imagery for the rebirth of Israel.

The creation psalms, which also begin at the same time (e.g. Ps. 104), or the text about creation in Gen. 1 at the beginning of the Bible, also speak about this *ruah* which makes life possible, which as a bond between heaven and earth, above and below, enables and sustains creation. Thus *ruah* does not depict a God who is enthroned above the earth, unmoved and unmovable, but a deity who binds heaven and earth together, who creates space for life by overcoming the abyss which separates and thus also making the future possible.

As language is not random but is connected with the reality in which it moves, it is important to emphasize the feminine background of experience to the Hebrew notion of the *ruah*. With the change of language, marked changes of content also came about: thus it was only at the frontier between the Old and New Testaments that the feminine concept *ruah* was transformed into the Greek neutral concept *pneuma*. In the course of the Christian tradition the notion was then rendered with the Latin masculine *spiritus*, and as *spiritus sanctus* was then personified as the third person of the Trinity. In this twofold work of translation not only was the term translated – translation is always more than merely transferring something into another language – but it was also introduced into other spheres of thought and imagination. Here some of the old experiential background was lost: for *ruah* is not simply identical with *spiritus* or our modern terms; the 'spirit' lost much of its life and vitality and was often no longer understood like the Hebrew *ruah*. But what was lost in language often continued to be preserved in symbolism. Thus even in the Christian sphere, the spirit was mostly represented by the dove, the age-old symbol of the deities of the ancient Near East. The feminine background is also often still recognizable in pictorial representations of the Holy Spirit – though often heavily distorted.[6]

As language always reflects the reality in which it takes place, the struggle for a fair language in talking about God, which no longer discriminates against women, is a decisive criterion by which we shall see how seriously the feminist criticism is taken.

Translated by John Bowden

Notes

1. Cf. Helen Schüngel-Straumann, 'Gott als Mutter in Hosea 11', *Tübinger Theologische Quartalschrift* 166, 1986, 119–34.

2. Hebrew *rehem*, a term which appears often in the OT in the form *rahamim* = mercy, and expresses this motherly compassion of God.

3. For more details cf. Helen Schüngel-Straumann, *Die Frau am Anfang. Eva und die Folgen*, Freiburg 1989.

4. Cf. Herbert Haag, 'Von Eigenwert des Alten Testaments', *Tübinger Theologische Quartalschrift* 160, 1980, 2–16.

5. Cf. in detail Helen Schüngel-Straumann, *Rûah bewegt die Welt. Gottes schöpferische Lebenskraft in der Krisenzeit des Exils*, SBS 151, Stuttgart, 1992.

6. The symbolism of *sophia* (wisdom), is rather different from the Hebrew concept *ruah*; it is often used in the late period as a translation of the Hebrew *hokmah*, in parallel to *ruah*. There are also texts which simply use the two feminine notions interchangeably (cf. Silvia Schroer, 'Die göttliche Weisheit und der nachexilische Monotheismus', in Marie-Theres Wacker and Erich Zenger [ed.], *Der Eine Gott und die Göttin*, Freiburg 1991, 151–82).

Negative Theology as Postmodern Talk of God

Erik Borgman

I never saw more impressive trees than the bare trunks in a newspaper photograph taken shortly after the Gulf War. The photograph was of Kurds who had fled from Saddam Hussein to the cold plateau in the north of Iraq. They were sitting there unprotected in the snow and the freezing cold. And amidst them stood bare trees, without leaves and without fruit, as though they were raising their branches in a wordless cry for help. What I shall be saying in this article about negative theology and, in connection with that, about atheism, is ultimately to do with the image of these trees.

For me there is a connection between this photograph and the strange story in the Gospel of Mark in which Jesus sees a fig tree and because he is hungry looks for fruit on it. When he doesn't find any, he says, 'May no one ever eat your fruit'. And as he says this, the tree, which was previously in full leaf, withers (Mark 11.12–14,20; cf. Matt. 21.18–19). Better a bare, dead tree which makes it clear that it has nothing to offer the hungry passer-by than that deceptive green! Just as later in the same story, Jesus prefers an empty temple court to a space where there are crowds and sacrifices, but no justice is done (Mark 11.15–17; cf. Matt. 2.12–13). He drives everyone away, echoing the outburst of the prophet Jeremiah. 'Will you steal, murder, commit adultery, swear falsehood . . . and then come and stand in this house, which is called by my name? Has this house, which is called by my name, become a den of robbers in your eyes? Behold, I myself have seen it, says the Lord' (Jer. 7.8–11).

I. Theology and atheism

If this story not only says something about their teacher, but is also an expression of the radical prophetic behaviour of the first generation of Christians, it is no wonder that in the Roman empire they were called *atheoi*, atheists. This charge did not simply mean that they theoretically denied the existence of the gods and therefore refused to take part in the cult. Rather, in their behaviour they showed a complete lack of respect for the social order guaranteed by the gods, for what had to be respected and what had not.[1] The pagan writer Celsus noted with a mixture of mockery and relief that according to the Christians one first had to break with the 'teachers of civilization, those with greater understanding and even the fathers', in order to take really valuable lessons in life 'from wooldressers, cobblers or washerwomen'.[2]

1. Rejected by the church

In the eighteenth and nineteenth centuries, atheism became a philosophical and political position. In the name of reason it criticized existing society, its view of the world and the image of God which provided a basis for this world-view. However, in this period Christians and their churches had completely lost any critical recollection of the early charge of atheism. They did not recognize the atheists of their day as being in any way their allies. These atheists attacked the God who was preached by the churches, seeking to unmask him as a fiction to perpetuate unjust conditions. In 1870 the First Vatican Council could not think of anything better than solemnly to condemn anyone who denied that God was the Creator and Lord of all things visible and invisible. In the second half of the nineteenth century, above all, the Catholic Church began to take shape as an authority on which the chaos of modernity had no hold and which could rescue the holy from the unrestrained criticism of critical social movements – especially socialism – and radical thinkers.[3]

2. 'As though there were no God'

Only in the period between the two world wars did some theologians begin to put the question in a broader historical and social framework. That eventually led to the official recognition by the Second Vatican Council in 1965 that 'atheism often develops out of a powerful protest against evil in the world, when the claim to absoluteness is illegitimately attached to particular human values, so that these are regarded as God'. Thus atheism is seen as a criticism of the idols and of those aspects of

Christian faith which have grown up in history and give themselves the features of idolatry. So there was a considerable shift between 1870 and 1965. But even in the view of Vatican II, atheism remained fundamentally a criticism of the church, faith and theology from outside the church, and also according to this council had to be reckoned 'among the most evil features of our time'.[4] Only the 'death of God' theology and the theology of secularization which arose in the 1960s went a step further and tried to make a positive connection between the Jewish and Christian traditions and modern atheism. They exposed 'atheism in Christianity' (Bloch, 1968) in order to trace the theological meaning of contemporary theoretical atheism, and above all the way in which people gave their life practical form *'etsi deus non daretur'*, as though there were no God (Dietrich Bonhoeffer, on Hugo Grotius).[5]

Many of the ideas put forward in this context were overtaken or subsequently proved to be naive, but the project itself remains worth while, particularly in a culture which is described as 'postmodern'. That means that the stories which give the culture a context quickly lose their influence, and existence can be described, in the words of the American author Douglas Coupland, as 'life after God'.[6] To talk of God in this context means to take up the age-old tradition of negative theology.

II. Negative theology

Anyone going through the inner cities of the Western world cannot avoid the impression that Jesus has many successors in his outburst of wrath against the fig-tree. They are full of broken trees, damaged road signs and vandalized telephone boxes. And there are graffiti everywhere. Everywhere there are signs of discontent with the prevailing situation, and to my mind just as many monuments to the desire for security and safety, for meaning and truth. These are signs of the fact that 'we have no holy names, words for meaning, significance, love, God'.[7] They are a monument to these names and to those who want to pronounce these names, simply by demonstrating the absence of these names and the frustration that that means.

1. Existential experience

So interpreted in a particular way, they are manifestations of a present-day negative theology, a theology which speaks of God by saying what God is not. This is a negative theology which does not consist in the rational arguments of professional thinkers, but in the overwhelming existential experience of large groups of people, namely that the divine, the holy, that which makes human existence worth while, is not present in our world. It cannot be experienced, nor can it be named, and that is a crying lack. In this situation the task of the theologian is to bring out in more detail the sense of lack and emptiness, including the protest which there is in this sense. For in it we are on the track of the divine given by which we must live.[8]

This is the sense in which in my view, professional theologians must do negative theology. Now there are thinkers – mostly philosophers – who call themselves or are called 'postmodern' in the broad sense, who have tried to think through the experience that all forms of meaning, old and new, fall short, and therefore need to be approached with scepticism, mistrust and unbelief. My view is that in princple there is an ambiguity in postmodern thought which is analogous to an ambivalence in the traditional idea of a negative theology.[9] I shall go into this twofold ambiguity by means of the work of two theologians: Pseudo-Dionysius the Areopagite and Thomas Aquinas.

2. Pseudo-Dionysius

What negative theology is has been demonstrated in a classic way in the treatise *On Mystical Theology*. Traditionally this is attributed to a certain Dionysius (cf. Acts 17.22–34), but it was probably written by an anonymous author in Syria in the sixth century. According to this Pseudo-Dionysius, negative theology is ultimately a method of coming to know something about God. Here the treatise uses a comparison with the way in which a sculptor works. Just as the sculptor carves away the pieces which conceal the image concealed in the statue, so human beings must also go to work to arrive at the image of the hidden God: all that hides him must be removed from thought (1025b).

This notion of the way to the knowledge of God reflects a very negative view of the reality in which human beings live. According to Pseudo-Dionysius, God is so far removed from this that he absolutely transcends any seeing, feeling and thinking (1001a). His negative theology is based on the conviction that 'the lights of beings conceal the dark primal light of the creator, which is nevertheless infinitely brighter' (1025c). He interprets the experience of God's not being present in the reality which we human beings inhabit as a sign of God's infinite transcendence over the world. The difference between God and the sphere in which we human beings live is so great that we can only experience the absence of God. Many centuries later, Nicolas of Cusa (1401–1464) went further in this spirit in arguing that not-knowing is characteristic of human beings as creatures directed towards God. In his view the consciousness of not knowing God (*docta ignorantia*) is the human form of knowing God.[10]

In regarding the protest of men and women against the way in which their world is ordered as an expression of an implicit negative theology, I do not mean that it exposes the unambiguous absence of God. In that case negative theology would be a preparation for an authentic encounter with God elsewhere. Many people have thought, and still think, that (post)modernity is in fact a chaotic and meaningless whole and that God can be encountered only outside it. They then look for God in nature, within themselves, in the museum or the concert hall, in intoxication or in religious experience as pure truth. And most of those who have learned to see that there are no places which fall outside the influence of (post)modernity think that it is impossible to encounter God at all. Unless – and that is the argument of postmodern philosophers like Jean-François Lyotard and Jacques Derrida – this is in the fact that reality is deeply impossible to grasp and fathom. It has an infinite number of faces, and any attempt to establish its characteristics succeeds only by repressing and forgetting many of them. In this incomprehensibility, which in fact demonstrates the fundamental ignorance of human knowledge, they see something indescribable and infinite, the divine.

Postmoderns seem to think that the divine can be defined only through its complete indefinability. Here they stand in the tradition of Pseudo-Dionysius and Nicolas of Cusa, against whose conception of negative theology the Jewish philosopher Franz Rosenzweig (1886–1929) objected that according to the biblical stories God is quite definite.[11] In these stories, and for example also in the many contemporary forms of liberation theology, God is the symbol of a power which changes reality, a power of liberation. Negative theology is something different from exposing God's absence. Negative theology expresses God's hiddenness or, more adequately, in the words of the Dutch theologian Kornelis Heiko Miskotte (1895–1976), is about God's presence as the 'presence of an absence'.[12]

3. Thomas Aquinas

I wrote earlier that the work of postmodern thinkers is ambiguous, ambivalent, like the concept of negative theology. It is in fact possible to give a completely different interpretation of the texts of Lyotard and Derrida. This makes it possible to read these texts as contributions to a negative theology in the sense that I have in mind here.

In that case the emphasis falls above all on the fact that their work is to a great degree dominated by opposition to established thought, to what everyone knows and what is generally recognized. For example, Lyotard applies himself to remembering what has been suppressed, what must be forgotten in order to give the illusion that reality is plain and can be read. He wants an anamnesis of what has already been judged by the dominant way of thinking and strives to write about the indescribable.[13] Derrida, too, concentrates his attention on what is excluded by texts and the thought-patterns that they lay down in order to arrive at coherence, and on the suggestion that meaning and truth are exposed there. He, too, brings out this unspoken and unspeakable element and arrives at a way of reading texts in which what these texts push to the margin is put at the centre.[14] 'The margin becomes the centre' seems to be an extremely succinct summary of the lines which Paul writes in the first Letter to the Corinthians to make clear the meaning of the message that the crucified Jesus has risen from the dead: 'But God chose what is foolish in the world to shame the wise, God chose what is weak in the world to shame the strong, God chose what is weak and despised in the word, even things that are not, to bring to nothing things that are' (I Cor. 1.27–28).

This brings me to the way in which Thomas Aquinas (1225/26–1274) takes up the tradition of negative theology.[15] Thomas, too, thinks that God's presence in the created world is not such that we can experience, know or say how God is in himself. However, we can make use of God's workings in the reality which surrounds us, look at it 'from the perspective of God' and so to some degree arrive at knowledge of God (*Summa theologiae* I, q. 7, art 1). As long as we live, we shall have to make do with this incomplete knowledge of God. According to Thomas, we do not know what God is, but only what God is not. But at the same time, some words express the incomplete way in which the creation shares in the perfection of the creator. Human beings can certainly never express what God is. However, at the same time, that to which some words finally point can in the real sense be found in God, and only in a derivative sense in God's creation (*Summa theologiae* I, q. 3, art 3). The statement 'God is good' does not tell us what God is, since the understanding that human beings have of good relates to the goodness which can be encountered in the world. But according to Thomas, the denial that God is bad must not simply be supplemented with the denial that God is good. At precisely this point his emphasis is different from that of Pseudo-Dionysius. According to Thomas, in the end it is more adequate to call God good than to call some creature good, since in the reality in which we live nothing is wholly good. True goodness in its fullness is always to be found only in God, but this goodness lies in the direction of what human beings experience in their lives as good and the goodness that they long for.

So for Thomas both the goodness that is present in the world and the goodness which is absent from the world are traces of God. In the knowledge of the good that people have by experience, they also show knowledge of God. Precisely in experience, it is clear that goodness is lacking from the world and that the goodness which belongs with God is just not present in the world. Thus the experience of goodness is in fact the experience of the 'presence of an absence'. There are barriers in our understanding of reality which make this reality point beyond itself and thus begin to speak of God. Negative theology removes these barriers. Negative theology denies the aspects of goodness which tie this concept to the existing word which can be directly experienced.

In this sense a vandalized traffic sign or a burnt-out car can be understood as an expression of negative theology: out of a longing for meaningfulness and goodness in perfection, they make it clear that what prevalent thought presents as 'good' is not good. Thus, indirectly and indeed in a negative way, God becomes visible as liberator.[16]

III. Essayistic theology

The Jewish philosopher Emmanual Levinas has suggested that the postmodern philosopher of Derrida above all exposes the violence of (post)modern culture, the way in which the war of all against all apparently comes to an end but in fact is continued with other means.[17] The one who is the strongest imposes the reality of his order, but in so doing gives the impression that reality itself is based on this order. Postmodern thinkers like Derrida (and, I would add, Lyotard) devote themselves to the liberation of the oppressed and to making the invisible visible in order to break through this imposed order, but here their ultimate aim seems above all to keep the mystery open. That which is excluded and kept silent about is not depicted for its own sake, nor seen as a trace of the hidden presence of a God with a face, who defines himself, who acts and liberates. Here there is an abiding difference between postmodern philosophy and what is ultimately obvious to us in talk about a negative theology.[18]

More is at issue here than an abstract theoretical question. Levinas philosophizes as a survivor of Auschwitz in the constant awareness that our century has experienced the ultimate fiasco of what passed for rationality and morality. It is simply not enough to expose the violence of ordering thought and to devote oneself to colourful difference of being. This has become clear to me in reading a collection of essays by Dževad Karahasan, a writer from Sarajevo who for the last six months has been living in Austria.[19] According to Karahasan, the chaos of a hundred thousand possibilities prevails in his land of chaos; the dominant idea is that everything is in principle interesting and worth the trouble, a murder as much as a flower. Here it is not a matter of demonstrating hidden and suppressed possibilities, since all the possibilities are already visible. In the world of Sarajevo and Auschwitz – and of all the other catastrophes – Karahasan and Levinas are quite clear that thought must choose, take sides with humanity and hope.

Theological thought must expose the marginal and hidden hope which despite everything remains alien and expresses itself, for example, in unjust protest. It is the task of the theologian to read the expressions of disgust and anger as expressions of a negative theology. They are signs of the abiding presence of the supportive force of goodness, which in the light of the biblical narratives can be called God, even if that is the 'presence of an absence'. Karahasan and also Levinas do that in the form of a story. I see a way of thinking which keeps strictly to the concreteness of human experiences, dilemmas and strategies of tradition as the one that is most adequate, and would therefore argue for an essayistic theology.[20] The story of the cursing of the fig tree in the Gospel of Mark and the cleansing of the temple are part of this theology.

This story begins with Jesus entering Jerusalem riding on an ass, while people strew their cloaks or green branches in his way and sing: 'Blessed is he who comes in the name of the Lord; blessed is the kingdom of our father David which is coming' (Mark 11.1–10). This is not so much an escort for a new king as an ancient vision which again has him entering a city which really needs to be dedicated to him. It is the vision that the king rides meekly and in lowly fashion on an ass, and that the last is thus the first, the vision of a new earth in which righteousness dwells (II Peter 3.13). It is a vision that subsequently clears the temple court and makes the fig tree wither. And it dwells in our midst in all those places where the absence of God so painfully comes to light.

Translated by John Bowden

Notes

1. E. Fascher, 'Der Vorwurf der Gottlosigkeit in der Auseinandersetzung bei Juden, Griechen und Heiden', in *Abraham unser Vater*, ed. O. Betz, Leiden 1963, 78–105; N. Brox, 'Zum Vorwurf des Atheismus gegen die alte Kirche', *Trierer theologische Zeitschrift* 75, 1966, 274–82.

2. Origen, *Contra Celsum* III, 55; see the whole section (III, 44–71).

3. See Vatican I, *Dei filius* (Denzinger, no. 3021). Cf. P. Thibault, *Savoir et pouvoir: Philosophie thomiste et politique clericale au XIXe siècle*, Histoire et sociologie de la culture 2, Quebec 1972; E. Poulat, *L'église, c'est un monde: L'Ecclésiosphere*, Paris 1986, 211–40, 'L'Église romaine, le savoir et le pouvoir; Une philosophie a la mesure d'une politique'.

4. *Gaudium et spes*, nos. 19, 21 (Denzinger nos. 4319, 4321); J. Ratzinger, in *Das zweite Vatikanische Konzil: Dokumente und Kommentare* III, ed. H. Vorgrimler (= *Lexikon für Theologie und Kirche²*, 13), Freiburg, Basel and Vienna 1957, 336–49; J. Figl, *Atheismus als theologisches Problem: Modelle der Auseinandersetzung in der Theologie der Gegenwart*, Mainz 1977, 31–81; cf. F. Padinger, *Das Verhältnis des kirchlichen Lehramtes zum Atheismus*, Vienna and Salzburg 1973.

5. K. Rohmann, *Vollendung im nichts? Eine Dokumentation der amerikanischen 'Gott ist tot Theologie'*, Zurich, etc. 1977; Figl, *Atheismus als theologisches Problem* (n. 4), 87–115.

6. Cf. D. Coupland, *Life After God*, New York 1994.

7. F. Hölderlin, 'Heimkunft' (1801), line 101: 'We must often be silent, there are no holy names'. Cf. *Ons ontbreken heilige namen: Negative theologie in de hedendaagse culturfilosofie*, ed. I. N. Bulhof and L.ten Kate, Kampen 1992, esp. 7–26.

8. Cf. H. de Vries, *Theologie im Pianissimo und zwischen Rationalität und Dekonstruktion: Die Aktualität der Denkfiguren Adornos und Levinas'*, Kampen 1989; J. Hochstaffl, *Negative Theologie: Ein Versuch zur Vermittlung der patristischen Begriffs*, Munich 1976.

9. See the research project 'Ambivalenties van de (post)moderniteit' by the Dominican Study Centre for Theology und Society (DSTS) at Nijmegen.

10. Cf. M. Alvarez-Gómez, *Die verborgene Gegenwart des Unendlichen bei Nikolaus von Kues*, Munich 1968; F. Maas, *Vreemd en intiem: Nicolaas van Cusa op zoek naar de verborgen God*, Zoetermeer 1993.

11. F. Rosenzweig, *Der Stern der Erlösung*, Frankfurt am Main 1921/1988, 15–16.

12. K. H.Miskotte, *Als de goden zwijgen*, Collected Works 8, Kampen 1983, 48; English translation *When the Gods are Silent*, London 1967.

13. Thus Lyotard in W. van Rijen and D. Veerman, 'An Interview with Jean-François Lyotard', *Theory, Culture and Society* 5, 1988, 277–310: 302; for this interpretation of Lyotard's work see D. Veerman and C. van Boheemen, *Postmodernisme. Politiek zonder vuilnisvat*, Kampen 1988; cf. also B. Reading, *Introducing Lyotard: Art and Politics*, London 1991, 86–89. For attempts at theological assimilation see G. Scobel, 'Postmoderne für Theologen? Hermeneutik des Widerstreits und bildende Theologie', in *Theologie die an der Zeit ist: Entwicklungen – Positionen – Konsequenzen*, Paderborn etc. 1992, 175–229; F. Maas, 'Een lichtere incarnatie; Lyotard en het Vergetene', in *Breuklijnen, Grenservaringen en zoektochten, 14 essays voor Ted Schoof*, ed. E. Schillebeeckx et al., Baarn 1994, 171–83.

14. Cf. S. Critchley, *The Ethics of Deconstruction: Derrida and Levinas*, Oxford

and Cambridge 1992, esp. 1–58; the adage 'What was at the margin comes to the centre' plays a part above all in J. Derrida, *Marge de Philosophie*, Paris 1972. Derrida goes into negative theology in *Psyche: Inventions de l'autre*, Paris 1987, 535–96: 'Comment ne pas parler'. For an attempt to interpret his thought as negative theology cf. I. N. Bulhof, 'Open zijn als een vorm van negative theologie; over Derrida', in *Ons ontbreken heilige namen* (n. 7), 91–124. Attempts have been made to use Derrida theologically, especially by M. C. Taylor, *Deconstructing Theology*, New York 1982; *Erring. A Postmodern A/theology*, Chicago 1984; cf. also K. Hart, *The Trespass of the Sign: Deconstruction, Theology and Philosophy*, Cambridge 1989.

15. The interpretation of Thomas given here is above all based on 'The Non-conceptual Element of Knowledge in our Knowledge of God according to Thomas Aquinas', in E. Schillebeeckx, *Revelation and Theology*, London 1967; cf. also W. J. Hill, *Knowing the Unknown God*, New York 1971; H. W. M. Rijkhof, 'Inleiding op Quaestio 13', in *Over god spreken: Een texst van Thomas van Aquino uit de* Summa theologiae (I, 2, 13), Delft 1988, 940.

16. I have interpreted the various forms of liberation theology – Latin American liberation theology, feminist theology and Black theology – as negative theology in this sense in my book *Sporen van de bevrijdende God: Universitaire theologie in aansluiting op Latijnsamerikaanse bevrijdingstheologie, zwarte theologie en feministische theologie*, Kampen 1990.

17. For what follows see E. Levinas, *Noms propres*, Montpellier 1967, 81–189, and the commentary in Critchley, *Ethics of Deconstruction* (n. 14), 146–9.

18. Derrida goes into the central difference between what he calls 'deconstruction' and negative theology in the same way. cf. his 'Comment ne pas parler' (n. 13), esp. 540–46, 557.

19. Cf. D. Karahasan, *Sarajevo: Portret van een in zichzelf gekeerde stad*, Amsterdam 1994, 68f. (original *Dnevnik selidbe*, Zagreb 1993).

20. This standpoint is worked out in my *Alexamenos aanbidt zijn God: Theologische essays voor sceptische lezers*, Zoetermeer 1994; for the idea of the essay that underlies this cf. T. W. Adorno, *Noten zur Literatur*, ed. R. Tiedemann, Frankfurt am Main 1981, 9–33: 'Der Essay als Form'.

III · The God of Life and the Gods of Death

The Divine in a Godless Society

Johann Figl

Experience of the reality of the divine is not independent of cultural and historical conditions, but has an essential connection with a particular historical and cultural situation. In this article I shall be discussing the question of the divine in a godless society. So I shall first outline the particular religious, social and ideological contexts in which the reality of the divine is articulated, the intellectual trends which open up or hinder access to the reality of the Absolute, understood in religious terms, for men and women of 'Western' culture. However, this must be done in the awareness that this cultural sphere is deeply interwoven with the history of atheism and secularization. So first of all we must investigate the form of atheistic criticism of religion and God which is related to Christianity.

Only against this background can we reflect appropriately on the way in which a society remote from God may experience the divine.

In so doing we shall be investigating the most important forms of religious groups or tendencies in the 'Western' cultural sphere.[1] First we shall consider the religious and ideological alternatives to Christianity, and then the Christian answer to godlessness in the present situation.

I. The form taken by criticism of Christian theism in modern godlessness

Against the background of the different forms of experiencing the reality of the divine in specific religions the urgent question arises: what effect does the current form of remoteness have on this possibility of experience? To answer it, we need a brief sketch of the phenomenon of godlessness. Here we should first note that modern godlessness does not take the form of a fundamental and general criticism of religion but is an expression of freedom from a specific notion of God or religion.

In the first place it rejects the transcendent, personal God of the monotheistic tradition which predominated in the culture shaped by Christianity, i.e. that culture in which modern atheism arose and developed its strongest influence. Atheism in this sense is specifically a phenomenon directed against Christianity: it is to be understood as a critical reaction (cf. Vatican II, *Gaudium et spes*, 19).

1. Criticism of the Christian God

In this perspective, what Nietzsche called the 'death of God' that has been proclaimed is primarily the death of the Christian God. The ideas of God in other religions and the ideas of a divine reality in a more general sense were not so directly affected by it, though the criticism of the Christian religion has often become the framework and model for criticism of non-Christian religions – including Eastern religions. But despite his radical negations Nietzsche still allowed the possibility of a divinization in which human beings glorify themselves (as e.g. in the Greek ideas of the gods). It is gratitude towards such gods which 'makes him wonder at the religion of the ancient Greeks'.[2]

Certainly we cannot argue from this that the classical atheistic scheme of Feuerbach or Nietzsche would have allowed the assumption of a transcendent reality (in whatever way that was imagined); they were beyond question decidedly anti-theistic and in this sense god-less schemes. But what can again indirectly be read off this openness towards a general anthropological way of talking about the 'divine' is the primary thrust of its criticism. It is from the negation of the Christian concept of God and the theistic understanding of religion that a quite specific constellation of problems arises in a 'post'-Christian situation.

2. A personal experience of God

So how far – despite the present-day godlessness – is the experience of the divine possible? Given the thrust of modern atheism this question can now be given a more differentiated answer: the criticism of religion has certainly made a personal notion of God and a clearly defined theism more difficult. A predominantly apersonal experience of the divine and the experience of an absolute reality remain possible. However, this is thought of in immanent terms. It either does not take up or abandons the strict concept of immanence distinctive of the monotheistic traditions. So presumably religious traditions without this specific background are more compatible with the modern post-theistic mentality than the traditional theistic notions.

But a further hypothesis can be put forward. Precisely as a result of the 'death' of the theistic God, the 'resurrection' of the divine (in the sense of a non-theistic experience) is indirectly and perhaps unintentionally prepared for. Thus the end of theistic religion opens up possibilities of a new type of religion not primarily orientated on the concept of God.

This helps us to understand why in the West today it is particularly the Eastern religions which find a particularly strong following, since in their higher forms they do not know a personal God. The same is true of mystical currents whose ideas of the divine reality relativize or overcome the dogmatic, philosophical and institutional fixations.

II. The opportunities for an alternative religious experience of the divine in the face of atheistic criticism

It is therefore consistent with the structure and the focus of the modern criticism of religion that those modes of religious experience are acceptable to modern men and women in which a more unstructured understanding of the divine predominates. In most recent times these are provided above all by new religious movements whose content is markedly orientated on Hindu and partly on Buddhist thought.

1. New religious movements

Syncretistic as they are, these movements often blur the clear contours of a conception of the Absolute. By virtue of their meditative practices they are related to mystical dimensions of experience. In these syncretistic and in part esoteric movements, on the one hand the atheistic criticism of Christianity seems to be blunted, as is shown by the biographies of some of the protagonists of esoteric thought and by the views themselves.[3] Despite the numerous ambivalent and sometimes antithetical statements of new religious movements about the self-understanding of modern men and women (e.g. about autonomy, self-determination, etc.), in the eyes of religious seekers these movements which emphasize the mystical element can communicate a 'post-theistic' and 'post-Christian' experience of the divine.

But there is also the older stream of non-institutionalized religion in modernity, especially since the Enlightenment. It articulates itself in philosophical terms and understands itself as a general religious feeling which transcends the individual religions or confessions. For this current at least, talk of the divine is a plausible mode of expression. Such predominantly theoretical approaches are one-sided and problematical because they are not related to praxis; they are not put into practice by a cult.

As a result, to some degree they remain voluntary and random. However, that is accepted in order to avoid a closer tie with religious institutions. The question is, though, whether a concrete experience of the divine can be communicated in these 'free' forms distanced from institutionalized religion; a shift into agnosticism cannot be ruled out. There can be a loss of religious experience, and that will already make talk of a divine reality problematical.

2. Buddhism

Of the non-Christian religions, primarily Buddhism has great possibilities of acceptance. In it, reality is grasped in a 'godless' way; for there is no idea of a creator God and personal deity, or of a theonomous ethic based on it, which is experienced as heteronomous. While it is inappropriate to follow H. von Glasenapp in calling Buddhism an 'atheistic religion', the exclusion of the topic of God does prove an advantage in an encounter with people who come from the Christian tradition and who have found questions associated with it (including moral and psychological questions) to be a burden.

Another attractive feature of Buddhism (and also of Hinduism) is its *de facto* tolerance, which confirms the modern self-understanding deriving from the Enlightenment. Furthermore, Buddhism shows a much smaller degree of religious institutionalization than the Christian confessions. So it is experienced as less of a burden and meets the need for freedom nourished by the critique of religion.

Taken together, the aspects mentioned go a long way towards explaining why the reality of the divine or the Absolute experienced in Eastern religions finds so great an echo in the West, although the West is characterized by remoteness from God and a criticism of religion.

III. The Christian experience of God in the face of godlessness

Given these religious alternatives, which are becoming increasingly evident in a cultural sphere stamped over many centuries by Christianity, the question becomes increasingly urgent: how is the Christian experience of God to be preserved and shaped in an environment remote from God? First of all we must look at the specific reciprocal relationship between the modern history of Christianity and atheism. For unlike other religions, it is only the Christian cultural sphere which has produced such a high degree of resolute atheism. Nowhere else is God denied so radically and passionately, and nowhere else have there been so many people who for various reasons have so resolutely turned away from practising their native religion.

1. Two dimensions

Two dimensions need to be distinguished in the motifs and arguments of modern anti-Christian criticism of religion. This protest fights on the one hand against the claims to social power in the Christian confessions and on the other against the religious ideas, especially an authoritarian picture of God, that seem to legitimate these claims to power. So anyone who wants to reflect on the experience of the divine appropriately in this situation created by the critique of religion must distinguish between an ethical-political and an ideological-theoretical aspect. In no way can we limit ourselves to the religious dimension, for this is most deeply interwoven with the anthropological understanding of ethics and society.

It will only be possible to communicate the experience of the divine reality credibly if this does not legitimate any repressive or authoritarian relationships – with reference to the individual or society. It is also necessary to take this politically relevant aspect into account for historical reasons: the representatives of Christianity have brought a great burden upon themselves through the misuse of political power. These acts of injustice, some of which were committed in the name of God, have often obscured the image of the divine reality; the rise of modern atheism cannot be understood outside this context. So anyone who wants to discuss the experiences of the divine in a godless time must go into the two aspects mentioned.

2. Overcoming the alienation between Christianity and modern culture

The difficulties associated with the experience of God can be solved only if the problems which have arisen in connection with the relationship between modern culture and church tradition are overcome. First of all the Christian communities must explicitly repudiate the unacceptable practices of the past.

Injustices must be conceded; a confession of guilt the beginnings of which were already expressed at the Second Vatican Council over the origin of atheism (cf. *Gaudium et Spes*, nos. 20, 21) is called for. But a confession of omissions and failures in the past will be credible only if similar attitudes are ruled out in the present.

Now questions about the modern human self-understanding are also under discussion. In particular the serious difficulties over questions of autonomy have led to persistent alienation. They have contributed to the rise of a widespread godless tradition in the Christian cultural sphere. The problematical relationship between general cultural or social views and specifically religious views has been consolidated. It cannot be the task of the church in this situation simply to adapt to the modern picture of human beings, which in fact is highly varied. Nor can the aim be the restoration of former conditions in an apologetic-fundamentalist attitude.

It is necessary, rather, to work through the misunderstandings and problems which have arisen in a process of alienation lasting for centuries. Only if this proves successful can we expect a new openness towards the religious answer of Christianity to the question of meaning. So in their theoretical self-understanding, the Christian confessions must reflect on those practices and forms which they owe to a past time and culture, which are neither essentially bound up with Christian faith nor have universally been accepted by the Christian tradition. Some of the topics to be mentioned here are: equal rights for women, a sense of democracy, the capacity and possibility of the religious communities to meet individual human needs or to re-evaluate earthly conditions.

A religion which evades this task will lose its significance for the concrete experience of present-day men and women; for if religious life does not refer to everyday praxis, it becomes a special sphere. It is forced to the periphery and thus becomes irrelevant. In that case the religions which came into existence in pre-modern times become the advocates of forms of inequality instead of contributing to the overcoming of discrimination. The God of a religion understood in this way is experienced as a God of injustice and oppression, not as a God of life and liberation, which God in truth is and is confessed to be.

3. Criticism of the theistic picture of God – the opening up of a mystical experience of God

As its name already indicates, the central thrust of the criticism made by atheism lies in its negation of the existence of God; more specifically a theistic image of God with a Christian stamp is rejected. A fundamental answer must be given to this criticism, since it touches the heart of the Christian religion. On the other hand its purifying, cleansing aspects cannot be denied. These are directed in particular against anthropomorphistic narrowness and must also be taken into account in the Christian sphere; for in the last resort they also serve the authentic notion of the 'God who is always greater', even in the Christian sphere.

This results in the questioning of a theism which has all too rigid a structure. Talk of God becomes talk of the divine; talk of the divine thus becomes more general, anonymous and indefinite. This development must not be neglected, since in it this divine, understood in more general terms, really is experienced.

The religions of revelation need also to reflect again on their own anthropological foundation, since it is particularly in this sphere that the discussion with the critique of religion has to be carried on.

Finally, given the godlessness of modernity, the question of the natural knowledge of God must be taken up in a new form; philosophical theology is required. Here, while the argument must be 'rational' (in traditional terms), a dimension must also be taken into account which transcends rationality in the limited modern sense: the authentically religious dimension of human experience.

But how can an elemental religious sense be communicated in a way which can be experienced? In the context of the present situation, namely a society which is *de facto* godless, mysticism seems to be a convincing way. Accordingly, it is a central task of Christianity once again to bring to life the mystical dimension under present conditions. So it is important to engage the modern self-understanding in dialogue with the insights of the great mystics. If this dialogue is carried out carefully, then it will at any rate provide the possibility of meeting the challenges of a divine interpretation of reality, for on the basis of such an experience the experience of absolute reality can be newly discovered and experienced in one's own faith tradition.

Such discoveries are of prime importance in the present-day situation of remoteness from God. It is not enough to communicate a general and undifferentiated experience of the divine. What is under discussion is the concrete experience of transcendent reality, i.e. an encounter with God or the divine which – in general cultural and individual biographical terms – is stamped by a specific religious tradition.

Translated by John Bowden

Notes

1. As I shall demonstrate in more detail in a longer article, the following four main groups come into question here: 1. traditional Christian confessions; 2. the non-institutionalized religion of modern philosophy and culture; 3. new religions and new religious movements; 4. non-Christian religions in the Western context.

2. F. Nietzsche, *Beyond Good and Evil*, German is in *Werke*, Kritische Gesamtausgabe, ed. G. Colli and M. Montinari, Berlin 1968, VI, 2, 68; cf. J. Figl, *Dialektik der Gewalt. Nietzsches hermeneutische Religionsphilosophie*, Düsseldorf 1984, 296f.; R. Bucher, *Nietzsches Mensch und Nietzsches Gott*, Frankfurt am Main [2]1993, esp. 262ff.

3. Cf. J. Figl, *Die Mitte der Religionen. Idee und Praxis universalreligiöser Bewegungen*, Darmstadt 1993, Ch. VI, 'Der Ambivalenz neuer Religiosität geegenüber der Moderne', 169ff., esp. 174ff.

The God of Life and the Revival of Religion

Pablo Richard

I. Official religion and popular religion

1. Two religious dimensions

Today it is clear that there is a revival of the religious and mystical dimension. However, this has nothing to do with official religion, but is a revitalization of the religious roots deep in the people. I suggest a distinction between two religious dimensions: official and popular.

In fact in Latin America, most people practise two religions, one official or institutional and the other popular and traditional. People declare officially in the census, for example, that they are members of the Catholic religion, they receive the main sacraments (baptism and communion), and may well live as practising Catholics. Nevertheless, these same Catholics simultaneously practise another religion. In the case of members of indigenous peoples, this is an ancestral religion. The Afro-American populations take part in African cults such as voodoo and candomblé. In most cases they take part in the practices of popular religion. In some cases the practices are more or less controlled by the church, but in other cases the cults are independent and syncretistic, and there is almost always a presence of occult religious practices (animism, magic, horoscopes).

Something similar is happening, too, with Christians of the other historic Protestant churches. The current return of the religious and mystical dimension has little to do with the official religions, but with those deep religious roots that reveal themselves on the margin of institutionalized religion and independently of it.

2. Simultaneously

The distinction between two religions or religious spheres is often accepted explicitly and consciously. In the meeting of Latin American biblical scholars held in Salvador de Bahia, Brazil, in June 1994 to study specific instances of the relationship between the Bible, religion and black culture, the black leader Albérico Paiva Ferreira was insistent: 'Christ is not in the *terreirò*' (the place where the Afro-Brazilian rituals of candomblé are celebrated, and by extension the community which celebrates them). This leader is a prominent and active member both of the candomblé community and of the local Catholic parish, and said firmly that he had no difficulty in being a member simultaneously of both communities.

Similarly, at the Second Congress of Indian Theology held in Panama in December 1993, a statement about Indian religion said: 'Christ comes later.' The Indian peoples lived for more than five thousand years with their own religion, and in the last five hundred years they have survived thanks to their own religion and, sometimes, despite Christianity. Today they accept Christ and his gospel, but simultaneously and quite consciously they affirm at the same time: 'Christ comes later.' The first and fundamental thing is Indian religion. Christ is still thought of as belonging to the official religion.

In the case of popular religion too, Christians often make a distinction between the religion they feel to be their own and the church's official religion. In popular religion it is the people who decide matters and control religion, through a very varied range of popular religious leaders, who clearly proclaim their autonomy and identity *vis à vis* the official church hierarchy.

3. Inside the historic churches?

The deep level of religion, different from the level of institutionalized religion, can in certain circumstances make its presence felt in a significant way within the historic churches. This normally happens when the local church does not have a centralized, authoritarian power structure, when there are church base communities and a vigorous participation of lay men and women in the church, when there is a genuine attempt to evangelize through cultures and in dialogue with indigenous and Afro-American religions.

One of the challenges for liberation theology has been precisely to carry out an evangelization at the deep level of people's religious feeling and through popular religion. In some places this has been done, and has been an important contribution to the emergence of an Indian theology, a Black theology and other liberating popular theologies, linked to popular religion. In other places or circumstances liberation theology has developed almost entirely within the churches. It may reach the more aware and committed sections of the grass-roots, but it still does not succeed in penetrating the deep and original religious level of the people. In this case the duality between theology and popular religion is not overcome. Another movement, inspired by liberation theology, is the so-called popular reading of the Bible (or pastoral or community reading of the Bible). This movement is really bringing about an evangelizing and liberating encounter between the deep level of people's religion and the biblical tradition of the churches. This achievement is due to the fact that the people are present in this community reading of the Bible, especially the poor, oppressed and excluded people, who are able to take control of the process of interpretation of God's Word. This process is embedded in the religious and cultural life of the people.

II. Some characteristics of popular religion

1. Four elements

I want to look now at the essential characteristics and constituents of the people's deep religious experience, which I have distinguished from the official or institutionalized religious experience. I want to pick out for the moment just four important elements.

(a) The body. Popular religious experience is essentially expressed through the human body: in dance, music, food, clothing and health. The body that participates in religious actions is a body that is clearly sexual and which lives the religious dimension in its sexuality.

(b) The community. Religious activity is profoundly communal: it creates community and seeks to strengthen it. In community all take part in and all enjoy the religious experience. There are disciplines and boundaries (for example between initiates and non-initiates), there are specific functions and offices, but there are no hierarchies and authoritarianism to crush the community. Religious experience is marked by solidarity, sharing and tenderness, expressed physically in embraces, kisses and community symbols.

(c) The cosmos. It is not just men and women who take part in religious experience, but the whole cosmos: sun, moon, the earth, trees, flowers, water, animals, stones, and so on. Everything is included in religious activity, and the cosmic and the human form a single family, in which the cosmic is not only symbolic but the very body of God.

(d) Woman. In popular religious celebrations, and in indigenous and Afro-American celebrations, women have a special leadership role. Women are included in prominent places in rites and sacred ministries.

2. A return to religious roots

The deep or popular religious experience differs clearly, especially in the four features mentioned, from institutionalized religion. Institutionalized religion is normally disembodied, desexed, anti-cosmic, individualistic, authoritarian and patriarchal. Through the four elements mentioned, the deep religious experience is able to integrate at a deeper level religion and culture, God and culture. In it, ritual, myth and the religious sense have more force and importance.

The revival of religion, or the return to religious roots, taking place today as a result of the crisis of modernity, also has all the features of popular religion that I have described. It is a religion linked to the body, to dance, to music, to food and sexuality. It is communal and cosmic, with a marked ecological element and participation by women in crucial roles. The more official religion represses the body and sexuality, isolates human beings from their relations as brothers and sisters with other human beings and with the cosmos, and becomes authoritarian and patriarchal, the more it alienates itself from popular religion and comes into confrontation with the revival of religion and the religious sense in today's world.

III. The crisis of modernity and the revival of religion

1. Concepts of religion

The crisis of modernity has brought with it the crisis of modern concepts of religion. Auguste Comte thought of religion as a primitive form of knowledge, prior to critical and scientific knowledge, and doomed to disappear. Karl Marx defined religion as the opium of the people, and as the heart of a heartless system: for him, religious pain was only the expression of real pain, and religion, in his view, would disappear when social contradictions were overcome. Sigmund Freud thought of religion as a disease, an illusion of neurotic minds seeking to overcome fear; a healthy mind would not need religion. Max Weber described religion as a phenomenon destined to disappear as a result of the irreversible process of rationalization and secularization.

Maybe in the modern period religion really was what these thinkers claimed, but the crisis of modernity also means a crisis for a particular form of religion and the renaissance of religion with specific characteristics. We are witnessing a resurgence of the religious dimension and of the religious sense, within popular religions which spring up alongside modern, institutionalized forms of religion. Religion is reappearing now, not as backwardness, a drug, pain or disease, but as sanity, protest and utopia, the source of a new energy and of a new form of symbolic and mystical knowledge.

2. Three essential features

The religion which is re-emerging out of the crisis of modernity has three essential features.

(a) Gratuitousness. Religion is a reaction against intellectual rationalism, against modern instrumental reason, against the pseudo-liberating mechanisms of science and technology, against the myth of the efficiency of unrestricted development, against the fetishism of power and prestige, against the religion of the market and the morality of making the maximum possible profit. The new religious experience, coming back now as modernity goes into crisis, is a religion based on grace and truth, opposed to the legalism and hypocrisy of the official religions; it asserts a belief in gratuitousness in the face of calculating bureaucracies, an awareness of being rather than the passions of possession and power, a philosophy of poverty and sharing against the logic of the market and profit. What we find emerging is a religion of gratuitousness, of grace and *agape* or disinterested love.

(b) Transcendence. The religion emerging out of the crisis of modernity is a reaction against all perverse spiritualism that defines itself as something beyond the body, beyond the cosmos or beyond history. It is a reaction against those views of the spiritual that repress the body, destroy nature and proclaim the end of history. The religion reviving with the crisis of modernity is now looking for a transcendence within the domain of the body, the cosmos and history; a transcendence that is not beyond history but beyond the oppression within history; a transcendence that is not beyond the body and nature but beyond death but within the body and nature. Transcendence is the overcoming of oppression and death within our history, with its human, bodily and cosmic dimensions. This definition of transcendence is set out magisterially in biblical texts such as Isaiah 65 and Revelation 21–22.

(c) Transparency. The religion returning with the crisis of modernity is a religion that seeks the presence of God directly in the reality of things and people without mediation by institutions, dogmas or hierarchies. As the rebel Job says prophetically, 'I had heard of you by the hearing of the ear,

but now my eye sees you' (Job 42.3–5). God is encountered in the direct transparency of the cosmos, the body and the community, beyond empirical data and the limits of tangible reality.

God is in the deep and hidden dimension of history, revealed in the transparency and luminosity of creation, is contacted more by the heart, the imagination, silence, activity and mystical vision than through reason and practical definitions.

IV. The revival of religion and the life of the poor

So far I have looked at the distinction between official religion and popular religion, and how popular religion is currently enjoying a vigorous revival. I also looked at some basic features of popular religion. We now need to look at what this means for the salvation of the lives of the poor in the Third World or, simply, at the credibility of God as the God of life in the Third World. The expression 'Third World' no longer makes sense, but I use it for the sake of convenience. I use it to mean the poor countries (almost all of Central and South Asia, and Africa and Latin America) and the poor in all countries, in other words, the poor and deprived 80% of humanity.

1. The world of the excluded

The reality of death growing apace in the poor countries and among the poor of all countries is a glaring fact today. The collapse of the historic forms of socialism in Eastern Europe has been followed immediately by the collapse of the dependent capitalisms of the South. What is now growing is a savage capitalism, in which the richest 20% of the human race have appropriated 82.7% of world income, 81.2% of world trade and 94.6% of loans; in addition they consume 70% of world energy and 60% of food (cf the report of the United Nations Development Programme, *Human Development 1992*). The world is coming together into a single free market economic system that concentrates wealth in the hands of a minority and produces a poor and deprived majority in the Third World, which itself is increasingly isolated, forgotten and disposable.

Two death-dealing trends are apparent in the new international 'order': the destruction of nature and the exclusion of the majorities. The neo-liberal banquet is marvellous, but there are very few guests, and the natural world is being constantly depleted. 'Exclusion' is a new phenomenon added to that of the poverty and deprivation that already exist. The excluded are those who do not fall under the logic of the market, whose deaths do not affect the efficiency and productivity of the system. Among the excluded there is a growth in social disintegration, family breakdown and violence (not just the violence of the system, but the violence of the poor against each other, men against women, adults against children, one ethnic group against another). Also on the increase are crime, the drugs trade and mass epidemics.

The Third World, as the world of the excluded, is considered at root as a threat, as a guilty victim that must be sacrificed, and as a world suffering systematic aggression, for 'humanitarian reasons', by the Western powers. All possible alternatives, critical theories and liberating utopias, are coldly dismissed and destroyed. Somalia, Rwanda, Haiti and Bangladesh are just some of the foretastes of the future waiting the Third World. This situation of the death of humanity and the cosmos raises again the question how we can believe in God as the God of life and as the creator God. What religion can emerge as a utopia and hope in such conditions of death?

2. Wealth in the Third World

The crisis of modernity, which began with the crisis of the historic Socialist regimes of Eastern Europe and continued with the failure of savage capitalism in the South, is felt from the Third World as a crisis of civilization: a crisis of the modern Western world and of its corresponding neo-Christendom. So-called post-modern culture is no more than modernity *in extremis*. The Third World is faced with a specific task, building an alternative world with its own cultural and religious roots.

The Third World is distinctly poor in weapons, money and technology, but rich in humanity, culture, ethics and spirituality. There is a wealth and identity in the Third World that is all its own, a reserve of humanity, culture and spiritual strength that could be the source of a hope and the basis for an alternative way of life, not just for the Third World, but for the whole world. We must stop seeing the Third World as a threat, and think of it as a source of hope. In this article it is impossible to examine all the economic, social and cultural possibilities of the Third World. All I shall examine is its moral and spiritual force, and the liberating possibilities of a revival of religion in the world of the poor.

3. Is there an alternative?

Economists and politicians claim confidently that there is no alternative to the current global free market system. This may be true, at least in the short term. But as theologians and believers we insist, just as confidently, that it is possible to build an alternative to the logic of the market: an alternative to the consumption-obsessed, individualistic and violent culture of the market, an alternative to the market's ethics of death, based solely on efficiency and profit, and above all an alternative to the idolatry of the market. I insist: I am not talking about an alternative to the market as such, but about an alternative to the cultural, moral and spiritual culture of the market.

We live in a free market economy, but we do not belong to the market; we follow Jesus' injunction to be in the world without belonging to the world (John 17.14–19) and without loving the things of the world (I John 2.15–16). The alternative is to live in the present system with a different culture, ethics and spirituality, consistent with our faith in the God of life. Of course, in order to be a real alternative, this must have an economic, political and social base.

There is no room here to discuss the viability of this base, but it is a reality in the Third World. I shall simply mention here the strength of the alternative social movements, the new historical protagonists, popular economy and alternative economic projects, the rebuilding of local or grass roots power, the revitalization of civil society, etc. At this economic political base a culture, ethics and spirituality of life is developing, an alternative to the logic of the free market system.

4. The importance of religion

If the alternative to the free market system is an alternative to the market's own cultural, ethical and spiritual logic, then the importance of religion in saving the lives of the poor and excluded in the Third World becomes clear; it is part of our identity at the deepest level. In fact, the great written religions are almost all Third World religions: Islam, Buddhism, Hinduism, etc., and especially Christianity, which originated in Galilee and today lives and grows especially in the Third World (there are more coloured Christians than white Christians). As I said, the Third World is poor in weapons, money and technology, but rich in humanity, culture and religion. The more the Third World is threatened with death, the more the poor majorities are developing all their moral and spiritual life potential to survive, resist and build new alternatives.

This explains and gives meaning to the revival of religion in the Third World, and not just any religion, but a popular religion at the heart of which there is hope, protest and utopia, a popular, not an institutional, religion expressed in the body, community, the cosmos and the participation of women. It is a religion reborn out of the crisis of modernity, with a liberating dimension of gratuitousness, transcendence and transparency. This religion enables us to rediscover God as the God of life, opposed to all idolatry, economic, commercial, political, technological, cultural or institutional. The return and revival of the religion of mysticism, at a time of a crisis of civilization, is thus a sign of hope and life; it is the response on the poor and excluded to the crisis and what encourages us to resist and fight that all may have life.

Translated by Francis McDonagh

The Church after the Change – in Hungary

The fall of Communism was certainly to be expected; the question was, when? Outside the prison walls some signs could have indicated the coming liberation. But the prisoners themselves were taken by surprise. The Catholic Church, along with its hierarchy, was perplexed by the freedom which it had received. For a while patterns of thinking and the mechanisms of control of the church by the state continued to govern its actions. Then, anxiously and cautiously, it began to take its first independent steps.

The desert produces a great abundance of plants and flowers after longed-for rain. It was the same with us. A tremendous variety of spiritual and cultural phenomena took on new force. There was chaotic, free, exuberant growth instead of deliberate, ordered development. It could cause anxiety and uncertainty. Soon the church felt the environment to be hostile. The church and opposition groups had been united in the face of dictatorship. Freedom unleashed differentiation. Unity crumbled.

In a painful process it was necessary to note two dangers to society. The ideology of the Communist dictatorship encouraged tendencies towards secularization. The undertow of consumerism is having a similar effect, now with increasing strength.

The leadership of the church had been and is late in recognizing the signs of the time. Answers have been ambivalent. It is as though in our complex and secularized world the church were attempting to win back its former role, in the garb and armour of past times. Adaptation to the new conditions will take time. The church and society do not speak the same language. Their terms are different; there is a time-lag between their styles. There are misunderstandings, conflicts, fights. The end-result is a bad feeling generally, both in society and in the church.

In the dying days of the dictatorship, society expected a lot, perhaps too much, from the church: morality and education, social and charitable support, and perhaps mediation in the economy. Both the expectations and the answers proved unreal and brought disillusionment. The church was incapable of reacting rapidly, and when it asked for finance for its actions, it made itself unpopular.

Even after the change, the financing of the church, whether out of its own resources or from elsewhere, is unresolved. Its contributions to the common welfare are being encouraged by the state. By an annual decision of parliament, a grant is being made for religious church activity; in other words, this depends on politics and the economic situation.

A law relating to the restitution of former church property recognizes that buildings should be handed back if they are intended for religious, cultural or charitable purposes. That also means that the legal owners (dioceses, communities, orders) are being tied to their former property and their former activity. And as these buildings now have other users, the requests for their return cause antipathy and disputes. There is a talk of a *Kulturkampf*, a cultural struggle, as in nineteenth-century Germany. The necessary refurbishment of these decrepit buildings swallows up large sums of money. Only occasionally is the decision taken to organize life within a new framework, without allowing the pre-Communist past to be the determining factor.

A majority of the church have the ideal and reality of the pre-war period before their eyes: a powerful and strong church, influential through its institutions. Attempts have been made to build such a church. A considerable number of people in society have found this effort threatening. They expected a church of mercy, reconciliation and love. A grotesque situation has developed. The church has been branded as greedy and obsessed with possessions. But at the same time it is expected to serve society without being paid, and to sacrifice everything for society. At any rate, the church is following the model of a state church. The experiences of the immediate past and the small Christian groups have not been evaluated. The Second Vatican Council's picture of the church has not been able to establish itself sufficiently, although everyone refers to it.

The development of a pastoral plan has been thwarted by the difference in ideas. The action of the church leaders is guided only by chance pressures and occasions. After the change one could have hoped for an open church, capable of dialogue. Today the restoration of authority and control and the safeguarding of the institution seem to have gained the upper hand. Everywhere the church is becoming more rigid. In what is already a complicated social situation this behaviour is causing alienation and provoking criticism. There are now not only anti-clerical voices in society but also voices which are hostile to the church.

The church is fighting in many spheres. With great difficulty it has won a place in the media, but it can only gradually fill this with attractive content. It is fighting for schools at all levels. A Catholic university and church colleges, schools and kindergartens, have come into being. However, in total they make up only three per cent of such institutions.

The Hungarian church has gradually entered into relations with the world church. It is receiving considerable material support from aid organizations, dioceses and individual institutions. This is readily accepted, as an exchange of experiences. Difficulties in understanding and also artificial scaremongering make people feel the need to guard against the spiritual influence of 'the West' and 'dangerous' Western theology. For Christians from the West who want to help the Hungarian church these are painful experiences.

In the years surrounding the change there were numerous initiatives from the laity, but these met with mistrust from church officials. Many were broken off in resignation. Catechetical training and theological study courses are available to the laity. But the dedication of those involved comes to grief on the predominantly clerical attitude here. So while there are many meritorious efforts in the church of Hungary, it is difficult for them to assert themselves in the contradictions which have been inherited from Communism.

There are no crisis strategies for the rapid decline in the number of priests, which is not being compensated for by the slight rise in the number of vocations. Overwork brings dangers for people and for health. It is urgently necessary to involve the laity. It is equally vital to change ways of thinking and picturing the church in the direction of a situation in which everyone co-operates on his or her own responsibility, and all work together as brothers and sisters.

The church is increasingly open to social responsibility. The harvest is rich in this area. And the economic and moral situation of the country makes the need for the social and charitable activity of the church ever more necessary.

The past years of the church in Hungary have led through struggles and efforts. God is teaching us through the challenges and incidents of history. Initially it has proved possible to strengthen the hierarchical order of the church, to create new institutions, and to revive the religious orders to new life. The church is struggling for its presence in the media and in education. It is aware of the many unfinished tasks. But it always acts in hope of the support of the Lord of History.

Asztrik Várszegi OSB, Bishop,
Archabbot of the Congregation of Hungarian Benedictines and Former Secretary of the Hungarian Conference of Bishops.

The editors of the Special Column are Miklós Tomka and Bas van Iersel. The content of the Special Column does not necessary reflect the views of the Editorial Board of Concilium.

Contributors

KNUT WALF was born in Berlin-Dahlem in 1936. After studying philosophy, theology, law and canon law in Munich and Fribourg, in 1962 he was ordained priest in West Berlin. He gained his doctorate in canon law at the University of Munich in 1965, and between 1966 and 1968 was a pastor in West Berlin. After his Habilitation in Munich in 1971, from 1972–1977 he lectured in church and state church law in Munich, where he was also Director of the Canonistic Institute. Since 1977 he has been Professor of Canon Law in the Catholic University of Nijmegen and since 1985 has also been Professor in the Theological Faculty in Tilburg, The Netherlands. More recent publications on church law and theology are: *Menschenrechte in der Kirche*, Düsseldorf 1980; *Stille Fluchten – Zur Veränderung des religiösen Bewusstseins*, Munich 1983; *Einführung in das neue katholische Kirchenrecht*, Zürich, Einsiedeln and Cologne 1984; *Kirchenrecht*, Düsseldorf 1984; *Vragen rondom het nieuwe kerkelijk recht*, Hilversum 1988; *Western Bibliography of Taoism*, Essen ³1992; *Tao für den Westen – eine Hinführung*, Munich 1989. He is regularly involved in *Orientierung*, Zurich.

Address: Bart Hendriksstraat 17, NL 6523 R E Nijmegen, Netherlands.

ANGELIKA MALINAR was born in Oldenburg in 1961. As well as studying Indology and philosophy in Tübingen she spent much time in India, gaining her MA in 1987 with a work on Indian aesthetics. In 1987–88 she worked in the Tübingen Purāṇa project and gained her doctorate in 1991 with *Rājavidyā: das königliche Wissen um Herrschaft und Verzicht. Studien zur Bhagavadgītā* (forthcoming, Wiesbaden 1995). Since 1991 she has been academic assistant at the seminar for Indology and Comparative Religion in Tübingen. Her interests are in Indian philosophy, the history of Hinduism, the epics and Purāṇa literature and modern Hindi literature. She has also written a number of articles and collaborated in several scholarly projects.

Address: Seminar für Indologie und vergleichende Religionswissenschaft, Münzgasse 30, 72070 Tübingen, Germany.

RUBEN L. F. HABITO is Professor of World Religions and Spirituality at Perkins School of Theology, Southern Methodist University, and Resident Teacher of the Maria Kannon Zen Center, Dallas, Texas, USA. Born in the Philippines in 1947, he served as a Catholic missionary and educator in Japan from 1970 to 1989. He finished doctoral studies in Buddhism at Tokyo University in 1978, and taught at Sophia University. He practised Zen under Yamada Koun Roshi, and was named Zen Teacher in 1988. His published works include *Total Liberation: Zen Spirituality and the Social Dimension*, New York 1989, and *Healing Breath: Zen Spirituality for a Wounded Earth*, New York 1993, as well as ten other books in Japanese.

Address: Southern Methodist University, Perkins School of Theology, Dallas, TX 75275–0133, USA.

DAVID TRACY was born in 1939 in Yonkers, New York. He is a priest of the diocese of Bridgeport, Connecticut, and a doctor of theology of the Gregorian University, Rome. He is The Greeley Distinguished Service Professor of Philosophical Theology at the Divinity School of Chicago University. He is the author of *The Achievement of Bernard Lonergan* (1970), *Blessed Rage for Order: New Pluralism in Theology* (1975), *The Analogical Imagination* (1980), and *Plurality and Ambiguity* (1987).

Address: University of Chicago, Divinity School Swift Hall, 1025 East 58th Street, Chicago, Ill. 60637, USA.

HERMANN HÄRING was born in 1937; he studied theology in Munich and Tübingen, where he worked at the Institute for Ecumenical Research from 1969 to 1980; since then he has been Professor of Dogmatic Theology at the Catholic University of Nijmegen. His publications include *Kirche und Kerygma. Das Kirchenbild in der Bultmannschule* (1972), *Die Macht das Bösen. Das Erbe Augustins* (1979), and *Zum Problem des Bösen in der Theologie* (1985); he was co-editor and editorial director of the *Wörterbuch des Christentums* (1985). He has also written on questions of ecclesiology and christology, in the *Tijdschrift voor theologie* and elsewhere.

Address: Katholieke Universiteit, Faculteit der Godgeleerdheid, Erasmusgebouw, Erasmusplein, 6525 H T Nijmegen, Netherlands.

LAURENT MPONGO is Dean of the Theological Faculty of the Catholic Institute of Yaoundé, Cameroons. His publications include: 'Pain et vin pour l'Eucharistie en Afrique noire?', *Nouvelle Revue Théologique* 108, 1986, 517–31; 'La célébration du mariage dans les religions africaines', in *La celebrazione cristiana del matrimonio. Simboli e Testi*, Studia Anselmiana, Rome 1986, 343–59; 'Vers un rite africain de la passion du seigneur', *Traditio et Progressio*, Studia Anselmiana, Rome 1988, 359–74; 'Vers une fête chrétienne des ancêtres africains', in *Pentecôte en Afrique* 14, 1993, 39–58.

Address: Institut Catholique de Yaoundé, BP 11628, Yaoundé, Cameroun.

BRUNO FORTE was born in Naples in 1949 and ordained to the priesthood in 1973; he gained his doctorate in theology in 1974 and in philosophy in 1977. He is Professor of Dogmatic Theology in the Pontifical Theological Faculty in Naples. He has spent long periods of research in Tübingen and Paris and is widely published in Europe and Latin America. A visiting professor in several European universities, he was the first lecturer at the Congress of the Italian Church in Loreto in 1985 and at the Fifth Assembly of the European Churches in Erfurt in 1988. Actively committed to the ecumenical movement, he is a consultant of the Pontifical Council for Promoting Christian Unity. His books have been translated into several European languages. Those available in English are: *The Church: Icon of the Trinity*, Boston 1991; *Prayers*, Boston 1992; *The Trinity as History*, Boston 1993; *He Loved them to the End. Theological Meditations on Love and Eucharist*, Boston 1993; *A Short Introduction to the Apostles' Creed*, London 1994.

Address: Pontificia Facoltà Teologica Dell'Italia Meridionale, Viale Colli Aminei 2, 80131 Naples, Italy.

FRANS MAAS was born in Turnhout, Belgium, studied theology in Amsterdam and gained his doctorate in Nijmegen with *God meemaken in mensentaal. Over de draagkracht van ervaring in geloof en theologie*, Tilburg 1986. At present he is teaching fundamental theology and spirituality in the Theological Faculty of Tilburg. He has written articles in *Tijdschrift voor Theologie*, *Tijdschrift voor Geestelijk Leven* and *Speling*, and published texts of Meister Eckart (*Van God houden als van niemand. Preken van Eckhart*, Haarlem [2]1985) and essays on spirituality (*Er is meer God dan we denken*, Averbode/Kampen 1989); with H. Blommenstijn he has edited an introduction to mystical theology (*Kruispunten in de mystieke traditie*, Delft 1990) and an introduction to the thought of

Nicolas of Cusa (*Vreemd en intiem. Nicolaas van Cusa op zoek naar de verborgen God*, Zoetermeer 1993).

Address: J. P. Coenstraat 64, 5018 CT Tilburg, The Netherlands.

PETER EICHER was born in Winterthur, Switzerland in 1943. He gained his PhD in Freiburg in 1976 and a doctorate in theology in Tübingen in 1976; since 1977 he has been Professor of Systematic Theology at the University of Paderborn and has trained as a speech therapist. His publications include: *Die anthropologische Wende*, Freiburg 1970; *Offenbarung – Prinzip neuzeitlicher Theologie*, Munich 1977; *Theologie. Eine Einführung in das Studium*, Munich 1980; *Bürgerliche Religion. Eine theologische Kritik*, Munich 1983; *Neues Handbuch theologischer Grundbegriffe* (4 vols.), Munich 1984–5 (new ed., in 5 vols., 1991); *Es gibt ein Leben vor dem Tod*, Munich 1991; *Wie kannst du noch katholisch sein?*, Munich 1993. He has also edited or co-edited several volumes.

Address: Kilianstrasse 30, D-33098 Paderborn, Germany.

HELEN SCHÜNGEL-STRAUMANN is Professor of Biblical Theology in the University of Kassel. She studied theology in Tübingen, Paris and Bonn and in 1969 became the first lay person to gain a doctorate in Old Testament at the Catholic theological faculty of the University of Bonn. Her publications include: *Der Dekalog – Gottes Gebote?*, Stuttgart ²1980; 'Gott als Mutter in Hosea 11', *Theologische Quartalschrift* 166, 1986, 119–34 (which has also appeared in English); 'Mann und Frau in den Schöpfungstexten von Gen. 1–3', in *Mann und Frau – Grundproblem theologischer Anthropologie*, Quaestiones Disputatae 121, Freiburg 1989, 142–66 (which has also appeared in English); *Die Frau am Anfang*, Freiburg 1989; *Ruâh bewegt die Welt*, Stuttgart 1992. She has been co-editor of the *Wörterbuch der Feministischen Theologie*, Gütersloh 1991; and, with T. Schneider, of *Theologie zwischen Zeiten und Kontinenten. Für Elisabeth Gössman*, Freiburg 1993.

Address: Schwedenweg 113c, D-34127 Kassel, Germany.

ERIK BORGMAN was born in Amsterdam in 1957 and studied theology and philosophy at the Catholic University of Nijmegen, where he also works as a researcher; he gained his doctorate with *Sporen van de bevrijdende God* (1990). He is now working for the Dutch Dominicans, researching the development of the theology of Edward Schillebeeckx in connection with his context. He is deputy editorial secretary of *Tijdschrift voor Theologie* and theological adviser to the 8 May Movement, and has published a number of articles on developments in theology. He contributed to *Disciples and Disciple: European Debate on Human Rights and the Roman Catholic Church* (ed. C. Van der Strichele et al., Louvain 1993) and has recently written *Alexamenos aanbidt zijn God: Theologische essays voor sceptische lesers*, Zoetermeer 1994.

Address: Palestinastraat 1A, NL 3533 EH Utrecht, The Netherlands.

JOHANN FIGL was born in 1945 and studied Catholic theology and philosophy at the universities of Innsbruck, Tübingen (where he gained his doctorate in theology) and Vienna (where he gained his doctorate in philosophy). He teaches philosophy and religious studies at the Linz Theologische Hochschule; he is Professor of the Study of Religion at the Catholic theological faculty of the University of Vienna and President of the Austrian Society for the Philosophy of Religion. He specializes in the philosophy of religion; religions in modern conditions; especially universal religious movements; and mysticism and atheism (above all Nietzsche), and has written many books in these areas.

Address: Institut für Religionswissenschaft, Freyung 6a, A 1010 Vienna.

PABLO RICHARD was born in Chile in 1939, and ordained priest in 1967. He has degrees in theology from the University of Chile and in scripture from the Pontifical Biblical Institute in Rome; he studied biblical archaeology at the École Biblique in Jerusalem and has a doctorate in sociology from the Sorbonne in Paris. At present he works in Costa Rica as Professor of Theology at the Ecumenical School of Religious Studies in the National University and as training co-ordinator for DEI, an ecumenical research centre devoted to the continuing formation of pastoral workers in Central America and the Caribbean. His latest book to appear in English is *Death of Christendoms, Birth of the Church* (New York 1988), and *Apocalipsis: Reconstrucción de la Esperanza* (San José 1994) is due to appear in English shortly.

Address: Apdo 389–Sabanilla, 2070 San José, Costa Rica.

Members of the Advisory Committee for Dogma

Directors

Hermann Häring	Nijmegen	The Netherlands
Johann Baptist Metz	Vienna	Austria

Members

Nazaire Bitoto Abeng	Yaoundé	Cameroons
Nedjelko Ancic	Split	Croatia
Rogério de Almedia Cunha	S. Joāa del Rei MG	Brazil
Ignace Berton OP	Rixensart	Belgium
Leonardo Boff	Petrópolis	Brazil
Paulo Carreiro de Andrade	Rio de Janeiro	Brazil
Anne Carr	Chicago, Ill.	USA
Fernando Castillo	Santiago	Chile
Yves Congar OP	Paris	France
Karl Derksen OP	Utrecht	The Netherlands
Severino Dianich	Caprona/Pisa	Italy
Josef Doré	Paris	France
Anton Houtepen	Utrecht	The Netherlands
Elizabeth Johnson CSJ	Washington, DC	USA
Maureen Junker-Kenny	Dublin	Ireland
Nicholas Lash	Cambridge	England
Matthew Paikada	Kerala	India
Tiemo Rainer Peters	Münster	Germany
Thomas Pröpper	Münster	Germany
Herwi Rikhof	Nijmegen	The Netherlands
Edward Schillebeeckx OP	Nijmegen	The Netherlands
Robert Schreiter CPpS	Chicago, Ill.	USA
Herbert Vorgrimler	Münster	Germany

Concilium

Issues of *Concilium* to be published in 1995

1995/1: The Bible as Cultural Heritage

Edited by Giuseppe Alberigo, Wim Beuken and Sean Freyne

Focusses on the Bible as a cultural rather than religious inheritance. First, it looks at the function of the Bible as a window on the Ancient Near East. Then it shows how the Bible has found a place in various fields of traditional culture. Finally, it examines the Bible in the context of cross-cultural and cross-disciplinary study.

030030 7   February

1995/2: The Many Faces of the Divine

Edited by Hermann Häring and Johann Baptist Metz

God is believed in, experienced and responded to in many ways. How can the one tradition be enriched by the insights of others without the disintegration of all traditions? What is at stake in belief in God? These are the questions tackled in this issue.

030031 5   April

1995/3: Liturgy and the Body

Edited by Louis Chauvet and François Kabasele Lumbala

This issue begins by considering the use of the body and the senses in liturgy; it then moves on to the relationship between the liturgy, the body and corporate memory; finally it looks at current problems raised by a more physical liturgy in modern society.

030032 3   June

1995/4: The Family

Edited by Lisa Sowle Cahill and Dietmar Mieth

Do the Bible and Christian tradition advance a particular form or forms of the family? How do they place the family in relation to religious commitment? What resources does Christianity provide for a reconsideration of the roles of family members, a critique of unjust relationships and a spirituality or theology of the family?

03033 1   August

1995/5: Poverty and Ecology

Edited by Leonardo Boff and Aloysius Pieris

03034 X   October

1995/6: Religion and Naturalism

Edited by John Coleman and Miklós Tomka

03035 8   December

Issues to be Published in 1996

Back Issues of *Concilium* still available

All listed issues are available at £6.95 each. Add 10% of value for postage.
US, Canadian and Philippian subscribers contact: Orbis Books, Shipping Dept.,
Maryknoll, NY 10545 USA
Special rates are sometimes available for large orders. Please write for details.

1965

1	Dogma ed. Schillebeeckx: *The very first issue*
2	Liturgy On the Vatican Constitution: *Jungmann and Gelineau*
3	Pastoral ed. Rahner: *The first issue on this topic*
4	Ecumenism: *Küng on charismatic structure, Baum on other churches*
5	Moral Theology: *Its nature: law, decalogue, birth control*
6	Church and World: *Metz, von Balthasar, Rahner on ideology*
7	Church History: *Early church, Constance, Trent, religious freedom*
8	Canon Law: *Conferences and Collegiality*
9	Spirituality: *Murray Rogers, von Balthasar: East and West*
10	Scripture Inspiration and Authority; *R.E. Murphy, Bruce Vawter*

1966

11	Dogma Christology: *Congar, Schoonenberg, Vorgrimler*
12	Liturgy: *The liturgical assembly, new church music*
13	Pastoral Mission after Vatican 2
14	Ecumenism: *Getting to know the other churches*
15	Moral Theology Religious Freedom: *Roland Bainton, Yves Congar*
16	Church and World Christian Faith v. Atheism: *Moltmann, Ricoeur*
17	Church History: *Jansenism, Luther, Gregorian Reform*
18	Religious Freedom In Judaism, Hinduism, Spain, Africa
19	Religionless Christianity? *Bernard Cooke, Duquoc, Geffre*
20	Bible and Tradition: *Blenkinsopp, Fitzmeyer, P. Grelot*

1967

21	Revelation and Dogma: *A reconsideration*
23	Atheism and Indifference: *Includes two Rahner articles*
24	Debate on the Sacraments: *Thurian, Kasper, Ratzinger, Meyendorff*
25	Morality, Progress and History: *Can the moral law develop?*
26	Evolution: *Harvey Cox, Ellul, Rahner, Eric Mascall*
27	Church History: *Sherwin-White and Oberman; enlightenment*
28	Canon Law - Theology and Renewal: *Hopes for the new Canon Law*
29	Spirituality and Politics: *Balthasar; J.A.T. Robinson discussed*
30	The Value of the OT: *John McKenzie, Munoz Iglesias, Coppens*

1968

31	Man, World and Sacrament: *Congar, J.J.Hughes on Anglican orders*
32	Death and Burial: *Theology and Liturgy*
33	Preaching the Word of God: *Congar, Rahner on demythologizing*
34	Apostolic by Succession? *Issues in ministry*
35	The Church and Social Morality: *Major article by Garaudy*
36	Faith and Politics: *Metz, Schillebeeckx, Leslie Dewart*
37	Prophecy: *Francis of Assisi, Ignatius of Loyola, Wesley, Newman*
38	Order and the Sacraments: *Confirmation, marriage, bishops*

Please send orders and remittances to:

SCM Press Ltd, 26-30 Tottenham Road, London N1 4BZ

Concilium Subscription Information - outside North America

Individual Annual Subscription (six issues): £30.00

Institution Annual Subscription (six issues): £40.00

Airmail subscriptions: add £10.00

Individual issues: £8.95 each

New subscribers please return this form:
for a two-year subscription, double the appropriate rate

(for individuals)   £30.00   (1/2 years)   . . . .

(for institutions)   £40.00   (1/2 years)   . . . .

Airmail postage
outside Europe +£10.00   (1/2 years)   . . . .

                                                Total . . . .

I wish to subscribe for one/two years as an individual/institution
(delete as appropriate)

Name/Institution . . . .

Address . . . .

. . . .

. . . .

I enclose a cheque for . . . . payable to SCM Press Ltd

Please charge my Access/Visa/Mastercard no.   . . . .

Signature . . . . .Expiry Date . . . .

Please return this form to:
SCM PRESS LTD 26-30 Tottenham Road, London N1 4BZ

CONCILIUM

The Theological Journal of the 1990s

Now available from Orbis Books

Founded in 1965 and published six times a year, *Concilium* is a world-wide journal of theology. Its editors and essayists encompass a veritable 'who's who' of theological scholars. Not only the greatest names in Catholic theology, but exciting new voices from every part of the world, have written for this unique journal.

Concilium exists to promote theological discussion in the spirit of Vatican II, out of which it was born. It is a catholic journal in the widest sense: rooted firmly in the Catholic heritage, open to other Christian traditions and the world's faiths. Each issue of *Concilium* focusses on a theme of crucial importance and the widest possible concern for our time. With contributions from Asia, Africa, North and South America, and Europe, *Concilium* truly reflects the multiple facets of the world church.

Now available from Orbis Books, *Concilium* will continue to focus theological debate and to challenge scholars and students alike.

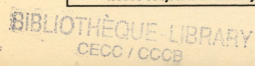